普通高等教育"十四五"规划教材
21世纪电子商务专业核心课程系列教材

新编电子商务英语

（第三版）

New E-Business English

(3rd Edition)

主　编　姚国章　王允曦　刘　伟
副主编　吴玉雪
主　审　翟丹妮

内容简介

本书结合电子商务专业教学的实际需要进行编写，选取具有实用性、新颖性和前瞻性的专业文章作为课文，进行全面的分析和讲解，帮助读者通过学习提高英语水平和研究电子商务专业的能力。本书分为电子商务概述、电子市场营销与电子金融、企业电子商务、行业电子商务、电子商务案例研究以及电子商务技术与安全6篇，每篇均包含2～3个单元，有详细的讲解和延伸阅读，读者可根据需要进行精读或泛读，从而进一步拓宽电子商务的专业和研究视野。

本书可作为电子商务专业本科、专科教材及相关专业硕士研究生英语教学用书，也可作为电子商务专业人员的参考用书。

图书在版编目(CIP)数据

新编电子商务英语 / 姚国章，王允曦，刘伟主编. —3版. —北京：北京大学出版社，2023.11
21世纪电子商务专业核心课程系列教材
ISBN 978-7-301-34597-9

Ⅰ. ①新… Ⅱ. ①姚… ②王… ③刘… Ⅲ. ①电子商务–英语–高等职业教育–教材 Ⅳ. ①H31

中国国家版本馆CIP数据核字（2023）第212040号

书　　　名	新编电子商务英语（第三版）	
	XINBIAN DIANZI SHANGWU YINGYU（DI–SAN BAN）	
著作责任者	姚国章　王允曦　刘伟　主编	
责任编辑	张玮琪	
标准书号	ISBN 978-7-301-34597-9	
出版发行	北京大学出版社	
地　　　址	北京市海淀区成府路205号　100871	
网　　　址	http://www.pup.cn　　新浪微博：@北京大学出版社	
电子邮箱	编辑部 zyjy@pup.cn　　总编室 zpup@pup.cn	
电　　　话	邮购部 010-62752015　发行部 010-62750672　编辑部 010-62754934	
印　刷　者	北京圣夫亚美印刷有限公司	
经　销　者	新华书店	
	787毫米×1092毫米　16开本　12.75印张　320千字	
	2008年6月第1版　2013年9月第2版	
	2023年11月第3版　2023年11月第1次印刷　总第11次印刷	
定　　　价	48.00元	

未经许可，不得以任何方式复制或抄袭本书之部分或全部内容。
版权所有，侵权必究
举报电话：010-62752024　电子邮箱：fd@pup.cn
图书如有印装质量问题，请与出版部联系，电话：010-62756370

第三版前言

自20世纪90年代中后期以来，电子商务经历了飞速的发展，对人类社会的进步和繁荣发展起到了巨大的推动作用。在当今时代，伴随着大数据、人工智能和5G移动通信等新一代信息技术的兴起，电子商务正迎来新的机遇和挑战。党的二十大报告指出，加快建设贸易强国，加快发展数字经济，促进数字经济和实体经济深度融合。电子商务既是促进贸易强国建设的有力武器，也是数字经济和实体经济有机融合的重要抓手，必将在实现党的二十大确定的目标任务中担当重任。更好地把握世界电子商务发展的大势，积极地拥抱电子商务的未来，是每位电子商务学习者和研究者的共同梦想。加强电子商务专业英语的学习、提升利用英语分析和研究电子商务的能力，则是电子商务学习者与研究者赢得未来发展机遇的重要选择。

在过去的二十余年中，笔者不但见证了电子商务在中国发展的奇迹，而且亲身参与了电子商务教学和研究的实践，尤其是在电子商务课程和教材建设方面一直在进行不懈的探索。《新编电子商务英语》第一版出版后得到了广大读者的认可，并被很多学校选用为电子商务专业英语教材。《新编电子商务英语》第二版出版后已被数十所高校选作教材。大家的支持给予了笔者极大的鼓励，笔者也因此坚定了为推进我国电子商务专业教育和专业人才培养提供更高水平的专业英语教材的信念。

《新编电子商务英语》第二版出版以来的数年中，笔者收到不少读者以及负责电子商务专业英语教学的教师的反馈，他们有的对书中存在的问题和错误予以指正，有的对新书的改版提出中肯的建议，有的还提供了新的教学参考资料。本书就是在充分吸收各方意见、建议的基础上完成的。比如，有的教师提出电子商务英语课程一般只安排32课时，很少能达到48及以上课时，原教材的内容过多，建议精简；有的教师提出原有的课后练习题题型较为单一且缺少参考答案，不利于教学，希望予以补充；有的教师提出书中课文中案例较少，内容缺乏对学生的吸引力，建议补充案例；等等。诸如此类的问题在本书中得到了很好的改进，希望能更加符合读者的期待。

本书包含电子商务概述、电子市场营销与电子金融、企业电子商务、行业电子商务、电子商务案例研究以及电子商务技术与安全6篇，每篇均包含2~3个单元。书中内容是有关国际电子商务发展的热点和典型案例，读者可根据需要进行精读或泛读。将本书作为本科教材使用时，建议课堂教学不少于32学时，48学时为佳，每一篇中可选择2~3个单元在课堂讲解，其余可安排学生自学。将本书作为专科教材使用时，建议教师适当增加课堂教学学时，同时组织学生进行自学。本书各单元生词的选取以是否超出大学英语四级词汇表范畴作为判断依据，没有出现在大学英语四级词汇表的生词，基本上都列在各单元的"Words and Expressions"中。

本书由笔者（南京邮电大学数字经济研究所所长、管理学院教授）联合吉林农业大学外国语学院王允曦副教授、刘伟副教授共同担任主编，我们的通力合作使得本书的专业化水平得以大幅度提升。吴玉雪作为本书的副主编，在资料的收集整理、英文课文的翻译等方面做出了很大的贡献。翟丹妮副教授对全书的内容做了全面的审阅，凭借扎实的外语功底和对电子商务的独到见解，提出了多方面的改进意见和建议。在此，一并向为本书成稿及出版付出努力的老师、同学和亲朋好友致以崇高的敬意和诚挚的谢意。

电子商务发展一日千里，新理论、新知识、新案例层出不穷，笔者最大的愿望是努力成为一名不落伍的"好学生"，受时间、精力、能力和水平所限，要做到这一点并不容易，但笔者坚信，和亲爱的读者一起去探索充满未知和希望的新领域，一定会收获满满、惊喜多多。

虽经多方努力，但本书难免存在不妥之处，敬请广大读者批评指正。

姚国章（yaogz@njupt.edu.cn）
2023年7月

本教材配有参考答案或其他相关教学资源，如有老师需要，可扫描右边的二维码关注北京大学出版社微信公众号"未名创新大学堂"（zyjy-pku）索取。

- 课件申请
- 样书申请
- 教学服务
- 编读往来

目　　录

Chapter 1　An Overview of E-Business ·· 1
第 1 篇　电子商务概述 ··· 1

UNIT 1　E-Commerce / E-Business in the New Economy ···························· 3
新经济下的电子商贸 / 电子商务 ·· 8
UNIT 2　Six Principles to Guide the Development of Global E-Commerce ······ 10
指导全球电子商务发展的六大原则 ·· 17
UNIT 3　The Internet of Things (IoT): Shaping the Future of E-Commerce ····· 21
物联网：塑造电子商务的未来 ··· 26

Chapter 2　E-Marketing and E-Finance ·· 29
第 2 篇　电子市场营销与电子金融 ·· 29

UNIT 4　Best Practices for Retail & E-Commerce to Win Consumers via Mobile Marketing ········ 31
零售和电子商务企业通过移动营销赢得消费者的最佳实践 ······················ 37
UNIT 5　What Is E-Marketing Plan ··· 41
什么是电子市场营销计划 ··· 47
UNIT 6　Customer Differentiation and Lifecycle Management of E-Marketing ··· 51
电子市场营销的客户差异化与生命周期管理 ·· 57

Chapter 3　E-Business about Enterprises ··· 61
第 3 篇　企业电子商务 ·· 61

UNIT 7　Challenges of Establishing Online Business in the E-Commerce Process Chain ··· 63
电子商务流程中建立网上业务面临的挑战 ·· 69
UNIT 8　How SMBs Can Profit from the Internet ···································· 72
中小企业如何从互联网中获利 ··· 77
UNIT 9　Could My Business Be an E-Business ······································ 80
我的业务能发展成电子商务吗 ··· 85

Chapter 4　　E-Business about Industries ·································· 89
第 4 篇　　行业电子商务 ··· 89

UNIT 10　　Retail E-Procurement: Minimizing Costs and Improving Productivity ······· 91
　　零售业电子采购分析：成本最小化，提高生产力 ··························· 95
UNIT 11　　Selling Products on Facebook: The Emergence of Social Commerce ········· 98
　　在脸书上销售产品：社交商务的出现 ·· 113
UNIT 12　　What Do Consumers Really Want? ·· 125
　　消费者真正想要的是什么？ ··· 129

Chapter 5　　E-Business Case Studies ·· 131
第 5 篇　　电子商务案例研究 ··· 131

UNIT 13　　Case Study of CRM: Securities Institute of Australia ······················· 133
　　CRM 案例研究：澳大利亚证券协会 ··· 139
UNIT 14　　Viral Marketing of Kettle Foods ·· 143
　　克特食品的病毒式营销 ··· 153

Chapter 6　　E-Business Technology and Security Issues ···························· 161
第 6 篇　　电子商务技术与安全 ·· 161

UNIT 15　　Some Technology Trends Affecting E-Business ································· 163
　　一些影响电子商务的技术趋势 ·· 168
UNIT 16　　E-Business Relies on Security ·· 171
　　电子商务依赖于安全性 ··· 178
UNIT 17　　UNCTAD B2C E-Commerce Index 2017 ·· 183
　　2017 年联合国贸易和发展会议 B2C 电子商务指数 ·························· 192

Chapter 1   An Overview of E-Business
第 1 篇   电子商务概述

- UNIT 1   E-Commerce / E-Business in the New Economy

- UNIT 2   Six Principles to Guide the Development of Global E-Commerce

- UNIT 3   The Internet of Things (IoT): Shaping the Future of E-Commerce

UNIT 1 E-Commerce / E-Business in the New Economy

TEXT

The Internet

A. E-commerce and e-business are both, products of the Internet. The Internet is basically a vast and ever increasing network of computers across the globe that are interconnected over existing telecommunication networks. Simply described, it is a, or the, network of networks. It is estimated that the number of persons connected to the Internet today well surpass 500 million, closing the gap on the 700 million or so connected to the telephone. It is calculated that there are over 90 million Internet hosts worldwide, facilitating a dramatic increase in the volume of trade and information available online. The economic rationale of the Internet comes from e-business and its developmental and moral platform will come from its impact in areas such as e-government.

Defining E-Commerce and E-Business

B. It is important to elaborate on the definitions of e-commerce and e-business as that will help determine the scope and perspective of this book. E-commerce has been simply defined as conducting business on-line. In the World Trade Organization (WTO) *Work Programme on Electronic Commerce*, it is understood to mean the production, distribution, marketing, sale or delivery of goods and services by electronic means. Broadly defined, e-commerce encompasses all kinds of commercial transactions that are concluded over an electronic medium or network, essentially, the Internet. E-commerce is a new way of doing business. It is transacting or enabling the marketing, buying, and selling of goods or information through an electronic media, especially the Internet.

C. From a business point of view, e-commerce is not limited to the purchase of a product. It includes, besides e-mail and other communication platforms, all information or services that a company may offer to its customers over the net, from pre-purchase information to after-sale service and support. There are essentially two major uses of e-commerce. The first is to use it to reduce transaction costs by increasing efficiency in the use of time and procedures and thus lowering costs. The other is to use it both as a marketing tool to increase sales (and customer services) as well as to create new business through it—for example, IT enabled business, call centers, software and maintenance services, etc. as well as digital commerce. It is thus a tool for both existing businesses as well as an opportunity for new business, both for existing companies as well as for new entrants.

D. E-commerce is seen as being B2C (business to consumer), B2B (business to business) and B2G (business to government). Of these three, B2B has been the most successful though recent reverses in the stock market valuations of high-tech stocks and the slowing down of the U.S. economy in particular is casting doubts on this. In future perhaps the major gains and usage of e-commerce and the Internet will come from new economy enterprises using it, governments using it (e-government), and social sectors using it (e-education and e-health).

E-Business

E. E-business is the application of Internet technologies to business processes. However, it is more than information technology tools or straight e-commerce. It also implies that the organization, especially its managers, are willing and receptive to radical changes that such new business techniques and tools bring. It implies organizational process and organizational culture re-engineering, for a true transition into the new economy. Its benefits come not just from the efficiencies and automation of a company's internal processes but from its ability to spread the efficiency gains to the business systems of its suppliers and customers.

F. An e-enterprise (participating in e-business) is defined as an enterprise prepared to conduct commerce in this new economy. This means it has created and embraced a business strategy formed by changing economics, new opportunities, and new threats. It has laid down the necessary technology infrastructure to support new business processes. It has used information technology to hone internal processes such as human resources, work flow management, and training.

Thus prepared, the enterprise is able to conduct e-commerce: the commercial exchange of value (money, goods, services, or information) between an enterprise and an external entity (an upstream supplier, a partner, or a down-stream customer) over a universal, ubiquitous electronic medium.

G. In order to appreciate the relevance of e-business and its potential to impact on business and development, it is important to understand that e-commerce and e-business are more than just electronics and commerce/business added together. They represent an entirely new way of doing business (including that of government) over a medium that changes the very rules of doing that business. They are therefore far more about strategy and management than they are about technology. In order to appreciate the importance of e-business, it is important to see it from the perspective of the transactional aspects of e-business, those that represent the business between the different players.

H. Therefore, e-business is taken as the extension of business on to the Internet; the re-engineering of business processes for digitizing of the transactions; the restructuring of the frameworks, both private and public to carry out the transactions seamlessly; and the development of the capacity in society and enterprises for this.

Conclusion

"E-commerce" can be understood in a narrow sense, and "e-business" can be understood in a broad sense. In this book, due to the wide range of text sources, there is both a narrow and a broad understanding, so "e-commerce" and "e-business" are not strictly distinguished.

Words and Expressions

surpass [sə'pɑːs]	vt.	超越，远远超出（预期）
rationale [ˌræʃə'nɑːl]	n.	基本原理，理论基础
encompass [ɪn'kʌmpəs]	v.	包括，围绕
entrant ['entrənt]	n.	新成员，参赛者
casting ['kɑːstɪŋ]	n.	铸件，铸造品
radical ['rædɪkl]	adj.	根本的，激进的
hone [həʊn]	n.	磨炼（技能），开发（产品）
ubiquitous [juː'bɪkwɪtəs]	adj.	无处不在的，随处可见的
upstream [ˌʌp'striːm]	adj.	逆流而上的；向上游的
seamless ['siːmləs]	adj.	无缝合线的，无伤痕的

Questions

Directions: *In this section, you are required to answer the following questions according to the information in the text.*

(1) How is e-commerce understood according to WTO Work Programme?

(2) What are the two major uses of e-commerce?

(3) Where do the benefits of e-business come from?

(4) What does the definition of an e-enterprise mean?

(5) Why can't e-commerce and e-business be described as just electronics and commerce/business added together?

Exercises

Directions: *In this section, you are going to read ten statements attached to the text. Each statement contains information given in one of the paragraphs in the text. Identify the paragraph from which the information is derived. You may choose a paragraph more than once.*

(1) E-business is taken as the extension of business on to the Internet and the re-engineering of business processes for digitizing of the transactions.

(2) E-commerce is transacting or enabling the marketing, buying, and selling of goods or information through an electronic media, especially the Internet.

(3) An enterprise which prepared to conduct commerce in this new economy has created and embraced a business strategy formed by changing economics, new opportunities, and new threats.

(4) E-commerce includes, besides e-mail and other communication platforms, all information or services that a company may offer to its customers over the net, from pre-purchase information to after-sale service and support.

(5) The economic rationale of the Internet comes from e-business and its developmental and moral platform will come from its impact in areas such as e-government.

(6) It is significant to understand that e-commerce and e-business are more than electronics and commerce/business added together.

(7) In future perhaps the major gains and usage of e-commerce and the Internet will come from new economy enterprises using it, governments using it, and social sectors using it.

(8) Broadly defined, electronic commerce encompasses all kinds of commercial transactions that are concluded over an electronic medium or network, essentially, the Internet.

(9) E-business implies organizational process and organizational culture re-engineering, for a true transition into the new economy.

(10) In order to appreciate the importance of e-business, it is important to see it from the perspective of the transactional aspects of e-business representing the business between the different players.

Translation

新经济下的电子商贸/电子商务

互联网

电子商贸和电子商务都是互联网的产物。互联网的本质是一个巨大的且不断增长的全球计算机网络,它通过已有的电信网络实现互联。简言之,它是一个由众多网络组成的网络。据估计,目前互联网用户已远超5亿,与大约7亿的电话用户数量相比,差距正在缩小。据统计,在世界范围内有超过9 000万台的互联网主机,使在线交易和有效信息量显著增长。互联网的经济原理来自电子商务,而它的发展平台和道德平台将来自在电子政务等领域的影响。

电子商贸和电子商务的定义

对电子商贸和电子商务定义的详细说明是非常重要的,因为它将有助于确定本书的范围和视角。电子商贸一直以来被简单定义为在线进行的业务。在WTO关于《电子商贸的工作方案》中,它被理解为采用电子化的方式进行生产、分销、营销、销售或交付产品以及服务。广义上讲,电子商贸包含通过某种电子化媒介或网络(实质上就是互联网)完成的各种商业交易。电子商贸是进行商业交易的一种新途径。它通过电子化的媒介特别是互联网实现交易,或者说它使产品或服务的市场营销、购买和销售成为可能。

从商业观点来看,电子商贸不仅仅局限于商品的购买。除了e-mail和其他交流平台外,它还包括一个公司可以通过网络提供给顾客的所有信息或服务,从售前信息到售后服务和支持。电子商贸本质上有两个方面的主要用途。第一个是通过时间和程序方面的效率提高来降低交易费用,以降低总成本。另一个是既把它作为增加销售(以及顾客服务)的一个营销工具,也把它用于开发新业务,例如,基于网络信息技术管理的业务,呼叫中心、软件、维护服务及数字商务等。它既是开展现有业务的工具,又是开展新业务的机会,对已存在的公司和新加盟者都是如此。

电子商贸被划分为B2C(企业面向个人)、B2B(企业面向企业)和B2G(企业面向政府)三种。在这三者中,B2B是最成功的,尽管股票市场上高科技股的市值下跌以及美国经济增长放缓使人们对此持怀疑态度。在将来，电子商贸和互联网的主要收益和用途将来自使用它们的新经济企业、政府（电子政务）和社会部门（电子教育和电子健康）。

电 子 商 务

电子商务是互联网技术在商业流程中的应用。但它不仅仅是信息技术工具或直接化的电子商贸，它还意味着组织，特别是组织的管理者乐意并接受这些新的商业技术和工具所带来的根本性变化。这是为了实现向新经济的真正转变而进行的组织流程和组织文化的再造。它的收益不仅来自公司内部流程的高效率和自动化，而且来自把这种效率收益扩散到它的供应商和客户的商业系统的能力。

一个（参与电子商务活动的）电子化企业被定义为准备在新经济条件下开展商业活动的企业。这表明它创造并拥有了一个由经济变革、新机会和新威胁形成的经营战略。它已经奠定了必要的技术基础来支持新的业务流程。它使用信息技术深化了内部流程，如人力资源、工作流管理和培训。经过准备，企业能够实践电子商贸：在一个企业和一个外部实体（上游供应商、合作伙伴或下游的客户）之间通过一个通用的、无处不在的电子媒介进行价值（资金、货物、服务或信息）的商业交换。

为了理解电子商务和它对于商业和发展产生影响的可能性之间的关联，重要的一点是要理解电子商贸和电子商务不仅仅是电子技术和商业/商务的简单叠加。它们借助改变处理业务根本规则的媒介，代表了一种全新的处理业务的模式（包括政府的业务处理）。因此，相对于技术来说，它们更多的是和战略与管理有关。为了理解电子商务的重要性，很重要的一点是要从电子商务交易方面的视角来看待它，这些方面代表了不同参与者之间的交易。

因此，电子商务可以看作商务向互联网的延伸，面向交易数字化的业务流程再造，为了实现无缝交易而进行的私有部门和公共部门框架的重构，以及社会和企业在这方面的能力的开发。

结 论

"e-commerce"可理解为狭义的"电子商务"，"e-business"是广义的"电子商务"。在本书中，由于课文来源广泛，对"电子商务"既有狭义的理解，也有广义的理解，因此对"e-commerce"和"e-business"不作严格区分。

Unit 2 Six Principles to Guide the Development of Global E-Commerce

Principle 1: Take a Cautious Approach to the Regulation

Take a cautious approach to regulation: Give global e-commerce some time to develop before determining which areas require government action.

There are two major threats faced by global e-commerce. One is rushing to impose legal and regulatory frameworks before gaining a full understanding of the issues and needs involved. Though it is easy to prejudge problems that governments might seek to solve, to do so at this early stage could be counterproductive. Cross-border business-to-consumer transactions represent a brand new pattern of trade, and the old ways of regulating trade will no longer work on the Internet.

The other threat, however, is doing nothing. Global e-commerce faces many "natural" barriers, including language, currency, and cultural differences; overseas transportation costs; and national brand identification. If nothing is done, the natural tendency for e-commerce is to "balkanized" into local zones, with consumers visiting only sites in their own country or a few where they feel comfortable. In order to fully realize the benefits of global e-commerce, governments should help when necessary to reduce the risks of cross-border transactions, but it will take time to determine when and where government action can help.

Unit 2 Six Principles to Guide the Development of Global E-Commerce

Principle 2: Increase Global Market Access

Increase global market access: Maximize opportunities for buyers and sellers to come together.

Empowering consumers and sellers—especially small enterprises—by expanding market access should be the main goal of any government action regarding global e-commerce. The reasons for this are basic, but very important.

First, a larger market reduces the marginal costs of operating Internet-based businesses, allowing companies to spread their fixed costs over more customers and thus lower prices. E-commerce will become more efficient and less costly by gaining global economies of scale. Greater market access also gives small entrepreneurial ventures a better chance of success: a comic book store at a local strip mall selling to nearby residents may have a hard time, because comic book buyers are a niche market and the number of customers is small, whereas an online comic book store selling around the world stands a much better chance in a larger customer pool. Low cost access to global markets is especially important for ventures in developing nations, which can use the power of global e-commerce to "leapfrog" their economic development efforts and sell to an array of wealthier consumers.

Second, a global Internet provides consumers with global choice. Shopping "bots" — automated buyer agents that seek out the best price on a given item—are increasing in popularity, and promise to bring tremendous efficiency to the pricing of goods and services on the Internet. Expanding the bot's range from national to international will encourage competition and reduce prices. Moreover, the Internet is not just a retailing channel—diverse services and media can be delivered over ever-expanding broadband networks, creating new business opportunities for communications, information, and entertainment ventures. Greater market access gives all these businesses, in whatever country they happen to be located, a better chance of success, and gives consumers of all nations a broader choice of goods and services.

Finally, as the infrastructure and systems to facilitate global e-commerce develop, access will also be increased in a more important market: the marketplace of ideas. History has taught us time and again that trade is the most powerful catalyst for cultural exchange and greater understanding between societies.

Principle 3: Don't Use Regulation for Protectionism

Don't use regulations for protectionism: Signatories to the World Trade Organization (WTO) or other multilateral trade agreements should not be allowed to impose rules on e-commerce or the Internet with the intent of reducing online foreign competition.

The practice of protecting domestic producers through the use of subtle or seemingly unrelated regulations is an old one, but the growth of global e-commerce provides the opportunity to take it to a new level.

As global e-commerce grows, the WTO will see more disputes about regulations aimed at the Internet and designed to give advantage to domestic industries. Examples include requiring websites to be delivered in the country's native language, requiring transactions to occur in the country's currency, requiring certain licenses or certifications to operate or use electronic equipment within the country, or requiring the use of nonstandard security protocols. Even more troubling is the process by which some of these regulations likely will be derived: the stoking of nationalistic fears that a country is being left behind in the new world economy. Countries that use such tactics might gain in the short run, but over the long run they will limit their standard of living and hinder global e-commerce. Rather than try to create rules and regulations to limit global e-commerce, nations would be better off pursuing policies designed to build a robust digital domestic economy.

Principle 4: Enforce Regulations Domestically

Enforce regulations domestically: Governments cannot impose their laws on foreign companies unless their activities fall within the government's territory or a treaty is in effect.

In the off-line world, activities engaged in by citizens of one country don't normally affect the citizens of another country unless those activities are specifically aimed at them (such as sending international mail). The online world should be no different. An online business based in one country cannot be expected to comply with the laws of other countries—such as privacy regulations or marketing restrictions—merely because their website is accessible in other countries.

On the other hand, if the Internet seller targets its goods or services to citizens of another country, that seller should be prepared to comply with the laws of that country. Put another way,

Unit 2 Six Principles to Guide the Development of Global E-Commerce

a government cannot "reach out" and exercise authority in another country, but it can exercise authority if someone in another country "reaches in" to consumers in its jurisdiction. Similarly, if two nations are part of a bilateral or multilateral trade agreement that imposes requirements on websites, then websites in both nations must comply with the terms of that agreement.

Principle 5: Limit Restrictions on Social, Cultural, and Political Content

Limit restrictions on social, cultural, and political content: Government restrictions on content cannot block trade in violation of WTO principles and must be enforced only within the restricting government's territory.

Given the wide variety of objectionable material available on the Internet, it is no surprise that some governments may seek to keep their citizens from accessing some content. Disputes in this vein are already arising for content that portrays or promotes racial hatred, violence, sexual activity, or drug use, to name a few. These issues go to the very heart of national sovereignty.

But if governments choose to exercise control over the foreign Internet content that their citizens may access, every nation must demand that every other nation adhere to two conditions.

The first is that such controls must apply only to cultural, social, and political content, not trade. Though the Internet will change the character of a portion of international trade transactions, there is no need to scrap the hard-won international cooperation that the WTO represents. Claims of cultural or political infringement should not be used as a back door method of discrimination against imports. If a country restricts global e-commerce on grounds that are (explicitly or implicitly) trade related rather than cultural or political, the WTO can and should take up the matter in the established dispute resolution process.

The second condition is that all content controls must be implemented domestically. In keeping with Principle 4 above, governments cannot "reach out" to shut down Internet operators that reside outside of their jurisdiction. Governments must control content through laws and regulations that apply to their own citizens, such as requiring Internet Service Providers to filter certain content or punishing individual users for downloading prohibited content. Of course, exercising control over every citizen's Internet behavior, while technically possible, requires control over the technology and communications infrastructure that only a few governments are likely to exercise. Inherent in the spread of Internet technology and the attendant economic benefits is a realization that the more time citizens spend in cyberspace, the less control their governments will have over them. This is why expansion of global e-commerce must be balanced with respect for sovereignty; if a government feels that the trade-off between commerce and social stability is not in its interest, the former is more likely to be rejected.

Principle 6: Take Advantage of Technology

Take advantage of technology: Encourage innovation in the development of technological tools and industry best practices that solve public policy problems.

Not every problem needs to be addressed by government regulation, especially with regard to the Internet. The Internet lends itself to creative solutions to policy problems precisely because software is a powerful tool to give people the ability to manage their own transactions.

Many technological solutions are being developed to facilitate an efficient and trusted environment for both buyers and sellers. One of the best examples is the Platform for Privacy Preferences Project (P3P). The project of the World Wide Web Consortium (W3C) is creating a system that allows browsers to look at a Web page's underlying source code to determine the privacy policy that covers the page; if the privacy level is below a predetermined level set by the user, the web browser (or other P3P implementation tool) will warn the user. This consumer-empowering technology, when fully implemented, may help alleviate the desire for strict government controls on data privacy practices and facilitate easier negotiation between nations with different privacy regimes. Technology promises other solutions as well, in areas from language translation to content control to dispute resolution.

Policymakers should turn to technology whenever possible and, more importantly, they should think in terms of what technology can do in the future rather than what it can do now. In order to facilitate the growth of global e-commerce, Progressive Policy Institute (PPI) makes the following proposals:

(1) Stay within the current international trade framework;

(2) Make the moratorium on tariffs for electronic transmissions permanent;

(3) Treat digitally delivered products as intangible goods;

(4) Eliminate tariffs on small-value transactions;

(5) Work with third parties seeking to provide solutions;

(6) Promote consumer education efforts; and

(7) Draft and enact global treaties governing criminal activity on the Internet.

Unit 2 Six Principles to Guide the Development of Global E-Commerce

Words and Expressions

counterproductive [ˌkaʊntəprə'dʌktɪv]	adj.	产生相反效果的，适得其反的
balkanize ['bɔːlkənaɪz]	vt.	使割据
leapfrog ['liːpfrɒg]	v.	超越，赶超
facilitate [fə'sɪlɪteɪt]	vt.	促进，使便利
objectionable [əb'dʒekʃənəbl]	adj.	令人不快的，讨厌的
sovereignty ['sɒvrənti]	n.	（国家的）主权，自主统治权
infringement [ɪn'frɪndʒmənt]	n.	违反，侵害
discrimination [dɪˌskrɪmɪ'neɪʃn]	n.	区别对待，歧视
alleviate [ə'liːvieɪt]	vt.	减轻，缓解
moratorium [ˌmɒrə'tɔːriəm]	n.	暂停，中止

Questions

Directions: In this section, you are required to answer the following questions according to the information in the text.

(1) According to the author, what should the government do to promote global e-commerce?

(2) Why is low cost access to global markets especially important for ventures in developing nations?

(3) According to the passage, how do some countries design regulations to give advantage to domestic industries?

(4) Why must expansion of global e-commerce be balanced with respect for sovereignty?

(5) What are PPI's recommendations?

Exercises

Directions: In this section, you are required to answer the questions with T or F.
T (for True) if the statement agrees with the information given in the passage;
F (for False) if the statement contradicts the information given in the passage.

(1) Though the Internet will change the character of a portion of international trade transactions, there is no need to scrap the hard-won international cooperation that the WTO represents.

(2) Cross-border business-to-consumer transactions represent a brand new pattern of trade, and the old ways of regulating trade will still work on the Internet.

(3) Instead of trying to create rules and regulations to limit global e-commerce, nations would be better off pursuing policies designed to build a robust digital foreign economy.

(4) The project of the World Wide Web Consortium (W3C) is creating a system that allows browsers to look at a web page's underlying source code to determine the privacy policy that covers the page.

(5) Global e-commerce faces many "natural" advantages, including language, currency, and cultural differences; overseas transportation costs; and national brand identification.

(6) As global e-commerce grows, the WTO will see more disputes about regulations aimed at the Internet and designed to give advantage to domestic industries.

(7) If governments choose to exercise control over the foreign Internet content that their citizens may access, every nation must demand that every other nation adhere to one condition.

(8) If the Internet seller targets its goods or services to citizens of another country, that seller should be prepared to comply with the laws of that country.

(9) History has taught us time and again that policy is the most powerful catalyst for cultural exchange and greater understanding between societies.

(10) Governments must control content through laws and regulations that apply to their own citizens, such as requiring Internet Service Providers to filter certain content or punishing individual users for downloading prohibited content.

Translation

指导全球电子商务发展的六大原则

第一个原则：对规则采取谨慎的态度

对规则采取谨慎的态度：在决定哪些领域需要采取政府行为之前，应当给予全球电子商务一些发展的时间。

全球电子商务面临着两大威胁。一个威胁是政府在完全理解相关问题和需求之前就匆忙地将法律与规范强加于它，尽管很容易预判出政府需要设法解决的一系列问题，但在早期介入很可能适得其反。跨境的B2C交易代表了一种新的贸易模式，因此老旧的管制交易规则在因特网上将不再适用。

另一个威胁就是政府不采取任何行动。全球电子商务面临着许多"天然"的障碍，包括语言、货币、文化的差异，海外运输成本以及品牌认可等。如果政府不采取行动，电子商务的自然发展趋势则是"巴尔干化"成一个个本地区域，即客户只去访问自己国家的网站或少数让他们感到舒适的其他国家的网站。为了充分实现全球电子商务的最大收益，在必要时政府应当伸出援手以减少跨境交易的风险，但必须进行长期研究，以决定政府行为在何时何地发挥作用。

第二个原则：增加全球市场准入

增加全球市场准入：使买卖双方交易接触的机会最大化。

在全球电子商务方面，通过扩大市场准入来增强客户和卖方（尤其是小型企业）的能力，应该是政府行为的主要目的。这样做的理由虽然很基本，但非常重要。

首先，更大的市场降低了基于因特网的业务运营的边际成本，这使公司可以把固定成本分摊给更多的客户，从而降低价格。通过获得全球规模经济，电子商务将变得更加有效和低成本。更大的市场准入也给小的风险型创业提供了更好的成功机会：一个位于商业街的面向附近居民的漫画店可能会度日艰难，因为漫画书的购买者是一个利基市场，客户数量非常少，而一个面向全世界销售的在线漫画书店面向的是更大的客户群，因而有更好的机会。低成本进入全球市场对发展中国家的企业尤为重要，这些企业可以利用全球电子商务的力量"跨越"其经济发展过程，并将产品销售给更富有的消费者。

其次，全球互联网给客户提供了全球性的机会。购物智能机器人（针对指定商品找到最优价格的自动化买方代理程序）越来越普及，并有望为线上商品和服务的价格机制显著提高效率。将智能机器人的搜索范围从国内扩大到国际，将促进竞争和降低价格。此外，互联网不仅仅是一个零售渠道——不断扩展的宽带网络可以提供多样化的服务和媒介，并为通信、信息和娱乐企业创造新的商业机遇。不管这些企业处在哪个国家，更大的市场准入机会都会带给它们更大的成功，并且使各国消费者在产品和服务的选择上有更大的余地。

最后，随着推进全球电子商务发展的基础设施和系统的建立，一个更重要的市场——概念市场也会增加准入。历史一再教育我们，贸易是促进不同社会间文化交流和理解的强力催化剂。

第三个原则：不要为保护主义使用规则

不要为保护主义使用规则：世界贸易组织协议或其他的多边贸易协议的签约国不应该为了减少在线领域的国外竞争而针对电子商贸或因特网施加过多管制。

通过使用微妙的或看起来似乎无关的规则来保护国内生产者的方式是很老套的，但是全球电子商务的发展提供了一个把保护主义推进到新水平的机会。

随着全球电子商务的发展，世界贸易组织将会面临更多的针对互联网以及旨在为本国产业谋利的规范的各种争端。例如，包括要求网站使用本国语言发布，要求用本国货币交易支付，要求在国内运营和使用电子化设备时有执照或证明，或要求使用非标准的安全协议。更麻烦的是，一些规则的产生可能是通过这样的过程：煽动新民族主义对于本国在世界经济中落后的恐慌。使用那些策略的国家可能在短期内受益，但是从长远来看，这将会限制它们的生活标准并妨碍全球电子商务的发展。因此，与其去努力制定制度和规则来限制全球电子商务，各国还不如制定政策以建立一个富有活力的数字化国内经济，带来的结果会更好。

第四个原则：强调规则国内化

强调规则国内化：政府不能强加法律给那些外国公司，除非它们的行为在政府的管制范围或条约约束范围之内。

在离线的世界里，一个国家公民的活动不会影响到另一个国家的公民，除非这些活动就是针对他们的（如发送国际邮件）。在线的世界应该也不例外，一个在线的企业不可能仅仅因为公司的网站在其他国家可以访问，就得遵守该国的法律（如隐私规则或者市场限制）。

另外，如果网络销售商把产品或服务定位于另一个国家的居民，那么销售商就要准备好遵守那个国家的法律。从另一个角度来说，一个政府并不能"伸手"在别的国家行使权力，但是如果另一个国家的某人"伸手"到它管辖的消费者身上，它就可以行使这种权力了。同样地，如果两个国家是双边或多边贸易协定的成员，而且这一协定对网站提出一定要求，那么这两个国家的网站都必须符合协议规定的条款。

第五个原则：限制对于社会、文化和政治内容的约束

限制对于社会、文化和政治内容的约束：政府对于内容的限制不能违背WTO的原则，妨碍贸易进行，并且必须只在政府管制范围内执行。

考虑到互联网上存在大量可以利用的负面材料，一些政府采取措施防止本国公民接触到这些内容也就不足为奇了。与描述或宣扬种族残害、暴力、性行为、毒品滥用等相关的内容已经产生了争议，这些问题已经深入国家主权的中心了。

但是如果政府选择对本国公民可能接触到的国外互联网内容进行控制，那么每个国家必须要求其他国家遵守两个条件。

第一个条件是这样的控制必须只适用于文化、社会和政治内容，而不涉及贸易。尽管互联网将改变一部分国际交易的特征，但没必要抛弃以WTO为代表的来之不易的国际合作。不应该把文化和政治侵权的主张作为歧视进口的非法途径。如果一个国家以（或明或暗的）贸易为由，而不是文化和政治方面的原因限制了全球电子商务，WTO就可以而且应该启动争端解决程序。

第二个条件是所有的内容控制必须在本国内实施。与上面的第4条原则保持一致，政府无权越界关闭不属于他们管辖范围内的网络运营商。政府必须通过适用于其公民的法律和规则来控制相关内容，如要求互联网服务供应商过滤一定的内容或者惩罚那些下载禁止内容的用户。当然，对每个公民的互联网行为实施控制，即使技术上可行，也仍要求超越技术和通信基础设施之上的控制，但这只有很少一些政府能够做到。与互联网技术传播相伴而生并且和经济利益同时出现的事实是：公民在网络上花的时间越多，政府对他们的控制就越少。这就是为什么全球电子商务的扩展与国家主权之间必须达到一种平衡。如果政府感到商业和社会稳定之间的权衡不符合其利益，前者更可能受到抵制。

第六个原则：利用技术

利用技术：在技术工具和产业最佳实践中鼓励创新以解决公共政策问题。

不是每个问题都需要政府的管制来解决，尤其是关于互联网的问题。互联网自身就是创造性的解决方法可以精确解决政策问题，因为软件是一种强大的工具，能给予人们管理自己交易的能力。

许多技术解决方法正在开发以促进买卖双方形成有效的、可信赖的环境。最好的一个例子就是个人隐私安全平台项目（P3P）。万维网联盟（W3C）的项目正在建立一个系统，这个系统允许浏览器查看网页底层代码以判断其隐私政策；如果这个隐私水平低于用户预先设置的水平，网络浏览器（或其他P3P实施工具）将对用户发出警告。这项用户赋权技术全面实施以后，可能有助于减少政府想要严格控制数据隐私的想法，并促进具有不同隐私机制的国家之间更容易地谈判。技术也为其他问题的解决提供了可能，包括语言的翻译、内容的控制以及争端的解决。

决策者们在任何时候都可以求助于技术，更重要的是，他们应该考虑的是技术在将来能做什么而不是现在能做什么。为了推进全球电子商务的发展，进步政策研究所（PPI）给出了以下建议：

（1）继续保持目前的国际贸易框架；

（2）对电子交易关税的延期偿付保持永久性；

（3）把数字化交易的产品视为无形产品；

（4）对低值交易取消关税；

（5）与第三方合作寻求解决方案；

（6）加强用户的教育；

（7）起草制定关于网络犯罪活动的全球性公约。

UNIT 3
The Internet of Things (IoT): Shaping the Future of E-Commerce

A. Besides computers, tablets and mobile phones, what other items in your home could be connected to the Internet? The answer might be far more than you can imagine: refrigerator, cupboards, coffee machine, washer, and many other household appliances. In March 2015, Amazon, the global e-commerce giant, unveiled to its selected Prime members a Wi-Fi connected Amazon "Dash Button" that could be attached to home appliances and allowed consumers to make online orders automatically by simply pushing the button. This innovation eliminated regular e-commerce shopping steps and made speedy and convenient online shopping possible. In July 2015, Amazon brought this "Dash Button" to all its Prime members for USD 4.99 each, accelerating the implementation and adoption of the IoT in the e-commerce sector.

B. Coined in 1999 by British technology pioneer Kevin Ashton, and evolved to the mainstream in the 2010s in both academic research and commercial applications, the IoT was defined as a worldwide information infrastructure in which physical and virtual objects were uniquely identified and connected over the Internet, enabling innovative, advanced services and creating a more convenient and smarter life. The IoT enhanced the connectedness of people and things on an unprecedented scale; Juniper Research predicted that the IoT would expand at an extremely high rate and that. These inter-connected devices would generate and communicate big data dynamically, enhance operational efficiency and create new business opportunities for various industries.

C. The e-commerce sector was no exception to the booming IoT development trend. The IoT would expand the scope and depth of e-commerce by linking people, smart devices and objects that were offline in the current e-commerce business model, generating unprecedented big data on product performance and customer behavior and experience, involving more communication and action, and ultimately shaping the future of e-commerce.

E-commerce Business Models

D. E-commerce, also known as electronic ecommerce, referred to commercial transactions conducted over the Internet, using website and mobile applications to make commercial transactions among manufacturers, merchants, retailers and customers. Since its beginnings in 1995 in the US, e-commerce had grown rapidly, generating a huge volume of transactions in the retail, travel and media businesses, and having an enormous impact on companies, markets and customers.

E. In recent years, with the advance of e-commerce technology, telecommunications and mobile smart devices, e-commerce platforms expanded from websites to mobile applications. By 2014, transactions over mobile applications accounted for growing revenues in the e-commerce sector. E-commerce would continue to grow rapidly in the coming five years. Manufacturers, merchants and retailers listed their products online in the form of an e-commerce website or mobile application with online shopping functionality. The website or application worked as an online shopping mall or shopping basket. Customers visited the website or used mobile applications installed on their mobile phones or tablets to select products, services and content they wanted, and then made orders online. The services or products would then be delivered to customers by electronic means or through delivery services. A flow of regular e-commerce shopping experiences was completed.

F. A business model was a series of planned activities aimed to generate profit for an organization in a marketplace. Professor Kenneth Laudon, in his book *E-Commerce 2015: Business, Technology and Society*, defined an e-commerce business model as a business model aimed to use and leverage the unique characteristics of the Internet and world wide web. Professor Laudon also stated that each successful business model, be it in the e-commerce or any other sector, must involve eight elements, namely, value proposition, revenue model, market opportunity, competitive environment, competitive advantage, market strategy, organizational development and management team.

G. In the current e-commerce scenario, competitive pricing, personalized recommendations and reduction of search and delivery costs generated value. E-commerce companies received revenue from online sales, transaction services and advertising services. Each e-commerce company had a marketplace with potential opportunities, but the marketplace was fiercely competitive. Companies planned market strategies to attract customers, but customers could move to competitors for future transactions.

Unit 3 The Internet of Things (IoT): Shaping the Future of E-Commerce

H. Over the past 20 years, although e-commerce had evolved to include additional elements such as mobile devices and applications, social networks, interactive marketing technologies, and personalized recommendations based on customers' previous online purchasing history on a given e-commerce website, online retail and services remained the greatest source of revenue growth in the e-commerce sector. The Internet connected customers' computers or mobile devices with online retail and service providers through an e-commerce website or mobile applications, but seldom connected other things or objects such as the products that a customer purchased, manufacturers, or the customers themselves. In addition, as was the case with traditional commerce in which retailers or distributors acted as intermediaries between manufacturers and customers, online retailers seldom gathered information about how a product fulfilled a customer's requirements after purchase, how the customer experienced the products and what improvements were necessary to enhance the quality and convenience of a product or service.

I. The IoT would link elements that were offline in the regular e-commerce model and involved more communication and action, allowing retailers and manufacturers to gather and analyze unprecedented amounts of data about consumer requirements, experiences and preferences. Thus, the IoT would enable retailers and manufacturers to provide personalized products and services to consumers and to act, virtually and digitally, as a customer's personal assistant.

J. Some observers predicted that the IoT would transform e-commerce in four ways, including optimized inventory management, location-based or real-time personalized recommendations, convenient shopping, and enhanced after-sale relationships, going far beyond current e-commerce transactions over websites and mobile applications.

Words and Expressions

eliminate [ɪˈlɪmɪneɪt]	v.	消除，淘汰
accelerate [əkˈseləreɪt]	v.	（使）加快，加速
implementation [ˌɪmplɪmenˈteɪʃn]	n.	贯彻；成就
dynamically [daɪˈnæmɪklɪ]	adv.	动态地
unprecedented [ʌnˈpresɪdentɪd]	adj.	前所未有的，无前例的
scenario [səˈnɑːriəʊ]	n.	设想，剧情概要
distributor [dɪˈstrɪbjətə(r)]	n.	经销商，分销商
intermediary [ˌɪntəˈmiːdiəri]	n.	调解人，中间人
virtually [ˈvɜːtʃuəli]	adv.	实际上，事实上
optimize [ˈɒptɪmaɪz]	v.	使最优化，使尽可能完善

Questions

Directions: *In this section, you are required to answer the following questions according to the information in the text.*

(1) What is the definition of the Internet of Things?

(2) What are the reasons for the expansion of e-commerce platforms from websites to mobile applications?

(3) How did Professor Kenneth Laudon define an e-commerce business model in his book?

(4) What is the difference between retailers or distributors in traditional commerce and online retailers?

(5) How would the IoT change e-commerce according to some observers' prediction?

Exercises

Directions: *In this section, there are five questions and for each of them there are four choices marked A, B, C and D. You should decide on the best choice.*

(1) What is the effect of bringing the "Dash Button" to all Amazon's Prime members for USD 4.99 each?

　A. Allowing consumers to make online orders automatically by simply pushing the button.

　B. Eliminating regular e-commerce shopping steps and made online shopping speedy.

　C. Accelerating the implementation and adoption of IoT in the e-commerce sector.

　D. Enabling innovative, advanced services and creating a more convenient life.

(2) What can customers do by using mobile applications installed on their mobile phones?

　A. List products online in the form of an e-commerce website or mobile application.

　B. Select products, services and content they wanted, and then made orders online.

　C. Ask merchants and retailers to deliver products, services and content they wanted.

　D. Share products, services and content they wanted online with their friend.

(3) Which item is not the source of e-commerce companies?

　A. Online sales.　　　　　　　B. Advertising services.

　C. Transaction services.　　　　D. Market strategies.

(4) What is the most important source of revenue growth in the e-commerce sector?

　A. Mobile devices and applications.　　B. Online retail and services.

　C. Interactive marketing technologies.　　D. Social networks.

(5) How does the IoT allow retailers and manufacturers to gather and analyze data about consumer requirements, experiences and preferences?

 A. By linking elements that were offline in the regular e-commerce model and involved more communication and action.

 B. By providing personalized products and services to consumers and to act as a customer's personal assistant.

 C. By connecting customers' mobile devices with online retail and service providers through an e-commerce website.

 D. By gathering information about how a product fulfilled a customer's requirements after purchase.

Translation

物联网：塑造电子商务的未来

除了计算机、平板电脑和手机之外，你家里还有什么设备可以连接互联网呢？答案可能远远超出你的想象：冰箱、橱柜、咖啡机、洗衣机和许多其他家用电器。2015年3月，全球电子商务巨头亚马逊面向其选定的金牌会员发布了一个能与无线网络连接的亚马逊"一键购物按钮"，它可以连接到家用电器上，消费者只需按下按钮就可以自动在线订购。这一创新省去了常规的电子商务购物步骤，使快速方便的网上购物成为可能。2015年7月，亚马逊以每人4.99美元的价格给其所有金牌会员提供了"一键购物按钮"，加速了电子商务领域实施和采用物联网的进程。

物联网于1999年由英国科技先驱凯文·阿什顿发明，并在2010—2020年间在学术研究和商业应用方面发展成为主流。物联网被定义为一种全球性的信息基础设施，其中真实物体和虚拟物体都可以被唯一标识并通过互联网连接，从而实现了创新的、先进的服务，并创造了更方便、更智能的生活。物联网以前所未有的规模增强了人与事物之间的联系；朱尼珀研究公司预测物联网将以极高的速度扩张。这些相互连接的设备将动态生成和连接大数据，提高运营效率，并为各个行业创造新的商机。

在蓬勃发展的物联网发展趋势中，电子商务也不例外。物联网将通过把当前的电子商务商业模式中处在非在线状态的人员、智能设备、实物对象连接起来的方式，扩展电子商务的广度和深度，产生关乎产品性能、客户行为和体验的前所未有的大数据，过程涉及更多的沟通和活动，最终塑造电子商务的未来。

电子商务商业模式

电商，即电子商务，是指通过互联网进行的商业交易，利用网站和移动应用程序在制造商、贸易商、零售商和客户之间进行商业交易。自1995年在美国产生以来，电子商务迅速发展，在零售、旅游和媒体业务中产生了大量的交易，对公司、市场和客户产生了巨大影响。

近年来，随着电子商务技术、电信和移动智能设备的发展，电子商务平台从网站扩展到了移动应用程序。到2014年，移动应用程序的交易成为电子商务行业收入增长的原因。电子商务将在未来五年内继续快速增长。制造商、贸易商和零售商以电子商务网站或具有在线购物功能的移动应用程序的形式在网上列出他们的产品。这样的网站或应用程序起到了一个在线购物中心或购物篮的作用。客户通过访问网站或使用安装在手机或平板电脑上的移动应用程序来选择他们想要的产品、服务和内容,然后在网上订购。然后,这些服务或产品将以电子方式或通过送货服务交付给客户。一个常规的电子商务购物流程就完成了。

商务模式是一系列计划好的活动,旨在为市场中的组织创造利润。肯尼斯·劳顿教授在《电子商务2015:商业、技术和社会》一书中,将电子商务模式定义为一种旨在利用互联网和万维网的独特特性进行经营的商务模式。劳顿教授还指出,每一种成功的商务模式,无论是电子商务或任何其他行业,都必须涉及八个要素,即价值主张、收入模式、市场机会、竞争环境、竞争优势、市场战略、组织发展和团队管理。

在目前的电子商务场景中,竞争性定价、个性化推荐以及搜索和交付成本的降低产生了价值。电子商务公司从网上销售、交易服务和广告服务中获得收入。每一家电子商务公司都有一个有潜在机会的市场,但该市场竞争激烈。公司制订市场战略的计划以吸引客户,但客户在未来的交易中仍有可能转向他们的竞争对手。

在过去的20年里,尽管电子商务在发展过程中包含了更多的附加元素,如移动设备和应用程序、社交网络、交互式营销技术以及基于客户以前在某一电子商务网站上的在线购买历史而制订的个性化推荐等,但在线零售和服务仍然是电子商务企业收入增长的最大来源。互联网通过电子商务网站或移动应用程序将客户的计算机或移动设备与在线零售和服务供应商连接起来,但很少连接其他事物或对象,如客户购买的产品、制造商或客户自己。此外,与传统商业的情况一样,其中零售商或分销商是制造商和客户之间的中介,在线零售商也很少收集关于产品在购买后是否满足客户要求、客户对于产品的体验如何以及需要进行哪些改进以提高产品或服务的质量和便利性的信息。

物联网将连接在常规电子商务模式中离线的元素,涉及更多的沟通和活动,使零售商和制造商能够收集和分析前所未有的、大量的有关消费者需求、经验和偏好等方面的数据。因此,物联网将使零售商和制造商能够向消费者提供个性化的产品和服务,并以虚拟和数字化的方式充当客户的个人助理。

一些观察人士预测,物联网将以四种方式改变电子商务,包括优化库存管理、基于位置或实时的个性化推荐、便捷购物和增强售后关系,这些将会远远超出目前通过网站和移动应用程序进行的电子商务交易。

Chapter 2 E-Marketing and E-Finance
第 2 篇 电子市场营销与电子金融

- UNIT 4 Best Practices for Retail & E-Commerce to Win Consumers via Mobile Marketing

- UNIT 5 What Is E-Marketing Plan

- UNIT 6 Customer Differentiation and Lifecycle Management of E-Marketing

UNIT 4
Best Practices for Retail & E-Commerce to Win Consumers via Mobile Marketing

A. Google defines mobile moments of consumers as micro-moments and divides them into "I want to know" moments, "I want to do" moments, "I want to go" moments and "I want to buy" moments. These micro-moments are crucial to marketers since they can be regarded as critical touch points within today's consumer decision making journey.

B. In each micro-moment stage, marketers should decide their mobile marketing and engagement tactics in order to "be there", "be useful", and "be quick".

Being There

C. Every marketer wants to "be there" for their consumers especially at their mobile moments. That's mostly because appearing in front of consumers at their mobile moments bring highest conversions for marketers. For instance, a joint study by Google and Ipsos study shows that 1/3 of smartphone users has purchased from a company or brand that provide information when they need it, other than the one they intended to buy from.

D. Being there gives a chance to brands to address consumer needs at the right moment, and help their consumers to move along their decision making journey. In addition, being there also helps marketers to deepen their relationship with their customers in order to increase their loyal customer base and increase lifetime values of their customers. Here are some mobile marketing insights and best practices for different mobile moments.

E. "I Want to Know" Moments

At "I want to know" moments, consumers are in exploring mode. At this micro-moment they want useful information and sometimes inspiration. For retailers, sending push notification when their customers are in store to provide further detail regarding products can be given as an example of being there at a "I want to know" moments. For e-commerce brands, in-App pop-ups that appear in front of customers who are searching for information within mobile App can be given as an example.

F. "I Want to Do" Moments

These are "how to" moments when people want help that's why at this micro-moment being there with the right content is crucial. For both retailers and e-commerce brands, mobile video advertisements targeted to "how-to" sentences related to products located in retail store and website can be used to "be there" at "I want to do" moments.

G. "I Want to Go" Moments

At "I want to go" moments, most consumers are looking for a local business or are considering buying a product at a local store. For retailers, mobile search advertisements targeted for specific locations can be used to increase foot traffic of retail stores. For e-commerce brands, similarly mobile search advertisements targeted for specific locations can be used to increase mobile site traffic.

H. "I Want to Buy" Moments

These are the moments when someone is ready to make a purchase and may need help deciding what or how to buy. For retailers, sending discount via push notification by using Beacon or other location sensing technology when consumer is at a retail store can be given as an example. For e-commerce brands, sending discount via push notification to a consumer who abandons his/her cart is an example of timely engagement.

Being Useful

I. For increasing the number of loyal customers, marketers need to do more than just "be there" at consumers' "I want to know", "I want to do", "I want to go" and "I want to buy" moments. Marketers need to "be useful" by providing relevant information when consumers need it. Thanks to increasing mobile usage, "being useful" is more achievable than ever.

J. Mobile technology provides a rich understanding of context to consumers' underlying intent and that context provides powerful clues for how brands can be most relevant and useful

Unit 4 Best Practices for Retail & E-Commerce to Win Consumers via Mobile Marketing

for consumers at their moments of need. Being useful at these moments are very important for marketers because if marketers can not provide utility to their customers, they can leave the brand forever.

K. For instance, according to Google and Ipsos, only 9% of consumers will stay on a mobile App if it doesn't satisfy their needs (for example, to find information or navigate quickly). In the following part, mobile marketing insights and best practices for different mobile moments such as "I want to know", "I want to do", "I want to go" and "I want to buy" will be put forward for retail and e-commerce marketers.

L. "I Want to Know" Moments

At "I want to know" moments, consumers are in exploring mode. In this micro-moment they want useful information and sometimes inspiration. For retailers, giving further information regarding products when consumers are in store by using Beacon technology can be given as an example for being useful. For e-commerce brands, in-App pop-ups that appear in front of consumers who are having hard time while navigating within App can be given as an example for being useful.

M. "I Want to Do" Moments

According to Google and Ipsos, 53% of smartphone users feel more favorable towards companies whose mobile sites or Apps provide instructional video content. For both retailers and e-commerce brands, adding instructional product videos to their mobile sites and/or Apps can be a way to "be useful" at the very moment when their customers are trying to understand the product.

N. "I Want to Go" Moments

According to Google and Ipsos, 61% of smartphone users say they're more likely to buy from companies whose mobile sites or Apps customize information to their location. For retailers, showing a nearby store where a particular searched-for product is in stock can be a good example for being useful at "I want to go" moments. For e-commerce brands, sending tailor made offers via interactive push notifications by targeting specific locations like malls, shopping centers, etc. can be used to catch consumers by being useful who are at "I want to go" moments.

O. "I Want to Buy" Moments

At these moments, customers should be empowered to purchase in whatever way suits their needs, whether in—store, on mobile, via call center or across devices. For retailers enabling mobile payment via NFC and for e-commerce brands enabling easy and quick payment with appropriate user experience within mobile App can be used as being useful tactics at "I want to buy" moments.

Being Quick

P. According to Google and Ipsos, 29% of smartphone users will immediately switch to another site or App if it doesn't satisfy their needs quickly (for example, they can't find information or it's too slow). In other words, for marketers, being fast is a crucial concept for both customer acquisition and retention plans. Mobile technology, particularly creates a behaviour change in consumers toward expecting speed in their relations with the brand in all channels including store, web, App, call center, etc.

Q. Google puts forward some different ways for brands to be quick in front of customers such as eliminating steps and anticipating needs. Marketers should deploy appropriate strategies in these areas in order to win micro-moments for their customers and/or prospects. Google's research shows that more than 1/3 of smartphone owners are usually in a hurry searching for a local business on their smartphone; 40% of them are usually in a hurry while looking for instructions on their smartphone and 28% of them are usually in a hurry while buying something on their smartphone. These numbers emphasize importance of being quick for retail and e-commerce sectors. The following part will give actionable insights for marketers in these sectors.

To be quick by eliminating steps, retail and e-commerce brands can deploy 3 strategies.

R. (1) Implementing one-click functionality: Both for retail and e-commerce Apps, adding "instant buy" buttons will enable consumers to finish their transactions quickly.

S. (2) Helping the user fill in forms: Both for retail and e-commerce Apps, one-click order will enable consumers to finish their transactions quickly.

T. (3) Providing alternatives to finish the transaction: For retail brands providing location based discount push notifications for directing consumers to retail store or for e-commerce brands sending interactive push notifications to the consumers who abandon their shopping basket will enable consumers to finish their transactions quickly.

To be quick by anticipating needs, retail and e-commerce brands can deploy 3 strategies.

U. (1) Putting the big stuff first: Both for retail and e-commerce, call to actions are one of the most important concepts. Retail brands can send location based push notifications with call to actions; e-commerce brands can use in App pop-ups containing call to actions that are triggered by specific user actions.

V. (2) Being location-aware: Both for retail and e-commerce Apps, communicating with target audience by using their location such as sending location based discounts with interactive push notifications will increase conversion rates.

Unit 4 Best Practices for Retail & E-Commerce to Win Consumers via Mobile Marketing

W. (3) Looking at past behaviour: Both for retail and e-commerce App, marketers can use push notifications according to their customers' past behaviors such as leaving an item in the shopping basket. Push notifications can be sent to these customers to enable them finish their shopping.

Words and Expressions

tactics ['tæktɪks]	n.	战术，策略
conversion [kən'vɜːʃn]	n.	变换，转变
joint [dʒɔɪnt]	adj.	共同的，联合的
notification [ˌnəʊtɪfɪ'keɪʃn]	n.	正式通知，正式告知
target ['tɑːgɪt]	v.	批评；把……作为攻击目标
navigate ['nævɪgeɪt]	v.	导航，确定……的航行方向
beacon ['biːkən]	n.	灯塔，指引者
empower [ɪm'paʊə(r)]	v.	授权，给……权力
retention [rɪ'tenʃn]	n.	保持，保留
trigger ['trɪgə(r)]	v.	引起，触发

Questions

Directions: In this section, you are required to answer the following questions according to the information in the text.

(1) Why does every marketer want to "be there" for their consumers especially at their mobile moments?

(2) What can be used to increase mobile site traffic for e-commerce brands?

(3) What will happen if marketers cannot provide utility to their customers?

(4) How should marketers do to win micro-moments for their customers and/or prospects?

(5) What will enable consumers to finish their transactions quickly?

Exercises

Directions: In this section, you are going to read ten statements attached to the text. Each statement contains information given in one of the paragraphs in the text. Identify the paragraph from which the information is derived. You may choose a paragraph more than once.

(1) Micro-moments are significant to marketers since they can be regarded as critical touch points within today's consumer decision making journey.

(2) Mobile technology, particularly creates a behaviour change in consumers toward expecting speed in their relations with the brand in all channels including store, web, App, call center, etc.

(3) Being there gives a chance to brands to address consumer needs at the right moment, and help their consumers to move along their decision making journey.

(4) Mobile technology provides a rich understanding of context to consumers' underlying intent and that context provides powerful clues for how brands can be most relevant and useful for consumers at their moments of need.

(5) The results from Google's research emphasize importance of being quick for retail and e-commerce sectors.

(6) According to Google and Ipsos, a majority of smartphone users say they're more likely to buy from companies whose mobile sites or Apps customize information to their location.

(7) Customers in search of information within mobile App can regard in-App pop-ups as an example for e-commerce brands.

(8) Both for retail and e-commerce Apps, communicating with target audience by using their location such as sending location based discounts with interactive push notifications will increase conversion rates.

(9) For retailers, mobile search advertisements targeted for specific locations can be used to increase foot traffic of retail stores.

(10) Marketers should deploy appropriate strategies in areas such as eliminating steps and anticipating needs in order to win micro-moments for their customers and/or prospects.

Unit 4 Best Practices for Retail & E-Commerce to Win Consumers via Mobile Marketing

Translation

零售和电子商务企业通过移动营销赢得消费者的最佳实践

谷歌将消费者的移动时刻定义为微时刻，并将其分为"我想知道""我想要做""我想要去"和"我想买"4个时刻。这些微时刻对营销人员至关重要，因为它们可以被视为当今消费者决策过程中的关键触点。

在每一个微时刻阶段，营销人员都应该决定他们的移动营销和参与策略，以此来做到"可用""有用"和"快捷"。

可 用

每个营销人员都想为他们的消费者随时提供服务，特别是在他们使用移动设备的时候。这主要是因为当消费者使用移动设备的时候出现在他们面前，可以为营销人员带来最高的转化率。例如，谷歌和益普索的一项联合研究显示，1/3的智能手机用户购买的产品不是来自他们想要购买的公司或品牌，而是那些在他们需要时提供信息的公司或品牌。

"可用"让品牌有机会在恰当的时刻满足消费者的需求，并帮助消费者进行消费决策。此外，"可用"还有助于加深营销人员与消费者的关系，以增加他们的忠实消费群，增加消费者的终身价值。以下是一些针对不同移动时刻的移动营销观点和最佳做法。

"我想知道"的时刻

在"我想知道"的时刻，消费者正处在探索模式。在这个微时刻，他们想要有用的信息，有时想要激励。对于零售商，当他们的顾客在商店时，通过推荐的形式为顾客提供关于产品的更详细的信息，可以被看作是在"我想知道"的时刻"可用"的例子。对于电子商务品牌商，针对顾客在移动应用程序中搜索信息时弹出商品视窗则被看作是电子商务中在"我想知道"的时刻"可用"的例子。

"我想要做"的时刻

这是当人们需要帮助时提供"如何操作"的时刻，这就是为什么在这个微时刻拥有"可用"的正确内容是至关重要的。对于零售商和电子商务品牌商来说，针对零售商店和网站产品的"如何操作"的移动视频广告，可以在"我想要做"的时刻为消费者做到"可用"。

"我想要去"的时刻

在"我想要去"的时刻，大多数消费者在寻找当地企业，或者正在考虑在当地商店购买产品。对于零售商来说，针对特定地点的移动搜索广告可以用来增加零售商店内的客流量。对于电子商务品牌商来说，指向特定网址的移动搜索广告可以增加网站的访问量。

"我想买"的时刻

这些时刻是有人准备购买商品，但可能需要别人帮助决定买什么或怎么买。对于零售商来说，当消费者在零售商店时，使用Beacon技术或其他位置感知技术，以推送通知的方式向消费者发送打折信息可以作为一个例子。对于电子商务品牌商来说，通过推送通知的方式，向放弃购物的消费者发送打折信息，就是及时参与的一个例子。

有　用

为了提高忠实客户的数量，营销人员需要做的不仅仅是在消费者"我想知道"的时刻、"我想要做"的时刻、"我想要去"的时刻、"我想买"的时刻"可用"。当消费者需要时，营销人员需要通过提供相关信息为消费者做到"有用"。由于移动设备使用量的增加，做到"有用"比以往任何时候都更容易实现。

移动技术为理解消费者潜在意图提供深入的背景，这种背景为品牌商了解如何在消费者有需要时与消费者保持最相关、最有用的关系提供有力的线索。在这些时刻做到"有用"对营销人员来说是非常重要的，因为如果营销人员此时不能向消费者提供实用的产品或信息，消费者可能会永远离开这个品牌。

例如，根据谷歌和益普索的调查结果，如果移动应用程序不能满足消费者的需求（如查找信息或快速导航），则只有9%的消费者会继续使用该移动应用程序。下面将为零售商和电子商务营销人员提出针对不同移动时刻——"我想知道""我想要做""我想要去"和"我想买"的移动营销见解和最佳做法。

"我想知道"的时刻

在"我想知道"的时刻，消费者正处在探索模式。在这个微时刻，他们想要有用的信息，有时想要激励。对于零售商来说，当消费者在商店时，通过使用Beacon技术为消费者提供更加详细的产品信息是做到"有用"的例子。对于电子商务品牌商来说，当消费者在应用程序中导航操作遇到困难时，在应用程序内弹出窗口可以被视为"有用"的例子。

"我想要做"的时刻

根据谷歌和益普索的数据，53%的智能手机用户对其移动网站或应用程序中提供教学视频内容的公司更有好感。对于零售商和电子商务品牌商来说，在他们的移动站点或应用程序中添加指导性产品视频，当客户试图了解产品信息时，也可以成为一种"有用"的方式。

"我想要去"的时刻

根据谷歌和益普索的数据，61%的智能手机用户表示，他们更有可能从设计出能根据客户位置定制信息的移动网站或应用程序的公司购买产品。对于零售商来说，提示在附近的一家商店里可以找到正在被寻找的商品是在"我想要去"的时刻"有用"的很好的例子。对于电子商务品牌商，通过定位商场、购物中心等具体地点，交互式推送通知，发送定制服务，让消费者觉得"有用"，以此来吸引在"我想要去"的时刻的消费者。

"我想买"的时刻

在这些时候，消费者应该有权以任何适合他们需求的方式购买，无论是去店里购买，还是以移动方式购买，或通过呼叫中心或跨设备技术购买。通过NFC技术实现移动支付的零售商，以及通过应用程序提供方便快捷的支付带来良好的用户体验的电子商务品牌商，都可以看作在"我想买"的时刻的"有用"的策略。

快　捷

根据谷歌和益普索的数据，29%的智能手机用户在他们的需求不能被即刻满足的情况下（例如，他们找不到信息或者太慢），会立即转到其他网站或应用程序。换句话说，对于营销人员来说，"快捷"是获取和挽留客户的关键因素。移动技术改变了消费者对速度的期望，消费者期望通过包括实体店、网站、应用程序和呼叫中心在内的所有可选择的渠道，与商家快速建立联系。

谷歌提出了几种不同的方式让品牌能够快速出现在消费者面前，比如减少购物步骤和预测消费者需求。营销人员应该在这些领域使用适当的策略，以便为他们的消费者或企业发展赢得微时刻。谷歌的研究显示，超过1/3的手机用户通常在自己的手机上急于搜索到本地企业，其中40%的人在手机急于搜索指令，28%的人在手机上急于购物。这些数字强调了对零售业和电子商务企业来说"快捷"的重要性。以下将为营销人员提供关于这几个方面的具有可操作性的建议。

通过减少步骤来实现快捷，零售和电子商务品牌可以采用二种策略。

（1）实现一键订购功能：无论是零售应用还是电子商务应用，添加"快捷购买"按钮将使消费者能够快速完成交易。

（2）帮助用户填写表格：无论是零售应用还是电子商务应用，"一键下单"都将使消费者能够快速完成交易。

（3）提供完成交易的选择方案：如果零售商能提供基于位置的折扣信息推送通知引导消费者到零售商店，或电子商务品牌能向放弃购物的消费者发送交互式推送通知，都将使消费者能够快速完成他们的交易。

通过预测需求来实现快捷，零售和电子商务品牌可以采用三种策略。

（1）把大宗商品放在第一位：对于零售业和电子商务来说，行为召唤都是最重要的概念之一。零售品牌可以发送基于位置的折扣信息的推送通知对客户进行行为召唤；电子商务品牌可以在应用程序中弹出由特定用户操作触发的行为召唤。

（2）位置感知：无论是零售应用还是电子商务应用，通过定位与目标客户进行交流，比如通过交互式推送通知的方式发送基于位置的折扣信息，都将提高转化率。

（3）参考历史行为：无论是零售还是电子商务应用，市场营销人员都可以根据客户过去的行为发送推送通知，比如客户把商品放在购物车里，就可以给这些客户发送推送通知，促使他们完成购物。

UNIT 5 What Is E-Marketing Plan

A. Let's begin by defining a marketing plan and then move onto defining its "new economy cousin" —the e-marketing plan. A marketing plan is a written document that details the current marketing situation, threats and opportunities, marketing objectives, and the strategies for achieving those objectives. A marketing plan can be written for each product, service, brand, or for the company as a whole. An e-marketing plan is a bit more focused than the traditional marketing plan. Although it often includes some of the same topics as a traditional marketing plan, it is more centered on the marketing opportunities, threats, objectives and strategies of the Internet.

B. The e-marketing plan defines your business model, builds commitment from all people who will be involved in its implementation, and establishes performance criteria and benchmarks for success. Development of your e-marketing plan begins with a complete review of your e-business model. What is a e-business model? In sections that follow, this text offers descriptions of e-business models. Review those descriptions and think about which one most closely describes your model. Before you begin an e-marketing plan, think about how to define your e-business model and how it influences your e-marketing plan.

E-Marketing Plan and Your E-Business Model

C. The e-marketing plan gives you a road map or a blue print to e-business success. The prerequisite to write a good e-marketing plan is a complete understanding of your e-business model. As you prepare your e-marketing plan, you may go through a learning process: you will analyze your e-business model in detail in an attempt to learn what drives your online sales and revenue streams.

D. What is your e-business model? Can you define it in a paragraph or two? A business model describes your architecture for product, service, and information delivery and sources of revenues (revenue streams). A business model identifies the value chain elements of the business such as inbound logistics, operations (or production), outbound logistics, marketing, service and support activities.

E. You must define your business model by writing your own description of it. From that description, can you identify each significant revenue stream and each potential revenue stream? Can you identify expenses that will be incurred in generating those revenue streams? Do you see the critical things that must be measured (metrics) and tracked to help assuring success? Can you see how your business model will use e-marketing to price, promote, sell, and distribute your product?

F. As you develop your e-marketing plan, you must think about how your e-marketing effort "fits" your business model. At a minimum, your business model will influence the way you forecast sales and predict e-marketing expenses. However, beyond basic sales forecasting and budgeting, there are aspects of your e-marketing plan that address the specific way you will do business, generate revenue, and consume resources. Your e-marketing plan should discuss how you will use information technologies to manage the marketing mix (product, price, place, and promotion), how you will plan to optimize your content, and how you will allocate resources to attract new customers, create loyalty with existing ones, and create revenue streams.

G. Be sure you define your business model before you write your plan. Can you identify your e-business model in the descriptive sections that follow?

Merchant Model

H. The merchant model is web marketing of wholesalers or retailers of goods and services. The goods and services might be unique to the web or an extension of a traditional "brick and mortar store front". This model includes catalogers who have decided to complement their catalog operation with a website or have decided to migrate completely to an online model. Benefits of this model include increased demand for goods and services via an entry into the global market, potential lower costs of promotion and sales, 24 / 7 ordering and customer service, and one-to-one custom marketing.

Auction Model

I. The auction model is web implementation of bidding mechanisms through multimedia presentation of goods and services. Revenue streams are derived from licensing of the auction technology platform, transaction fees, and advertising.

Manufacturer Model

J. The manufacturer model uses the web to compress the distribution channel so that rather than use intermediaries to get your products and services to market, you go direct to the customer via the web. For example, Dell Computer Corporation, maker of personal computer systems, uses this model by selling direct to consumers via their website. About 50 percent of Dell's sales are Web-enabled.

Affiliate Model

K. The affiliate model is a "pay for performance model". Revenue streams are created when customers click through links or banner advertisements to purchase goods and services. Affiliate marketing is when one website (the affiliate) promotes another website's products or services (the merchant) in exchange for a commission. The affiliate earns a commission (i.c., 10% of the purchase) while the merchant derives a sale from an affiliate (partner website). Through affiliate marketing, merchants can place their advertising banners and links on content sites worldwide and only pay a commission when those links generate a sale or a qualified lead. Affiliated content sites can convert their online content into e-commerce by populating it with these revenue-generating links.

Advertising Model

L. Like a traditional broadcaster or news media business models, the web advertising model provides content and services (i.e., e-mail, chat, forums, auctions, etc.) supported by banner advertisements and other forms of online advertising (perhaps e-mail newsletter advertisements). Some advertising models are called portals (i.e., AOL, Yahoo, and AltaVista) while others are called "free models".

Infomediary Model

M. This is a web model whereby the infomediary collects data from users and sells the information to other businesses. Traffic is driven to the infomediary's site by free offers (such as free Internet access or free hardware).

Subscription Model

N. In a subscription model, users pay for access to the site and the high value content that they view. Some models offer free content with premium content available only to paid subscribers. Advertising revenues may also be part of the revenue stream.

Brokerage Model

O. A brokerage model is a web market maker that brings buyers and sellers together. The model ranges from virtual malls to online stock and bond traders and can include business-to-business(B2B), business-to-consumer(B2C), and consumer-to-consumer(C2C). Transaction fees or commissions generate the revenue under this model.

Virtual Communities Model

P. The virtual communities model facilitates the online interaction of a community of users (members, customers, partners, students, etc.). The model makes it easy for the community members to add their own content to the online community website. Revenue streams are generated from membership fees and advertising revenue.

Logistics Model

Q. A business that utilizes the Internet to help other businesses manage logistical functions such as electronic payments, ordering systems, and shipping services in operating under the logistics model. Fees are the basis for the revenue scheme.

E-Business Models and E-Marketing Plan

R. What is the relationship between e-business models and e-marketing? Central problems to all the models identified in the previous section are three issues as follows:

(1) For these models to work, e-marketing planning is critical.

(2) These models generate tremendous amounts of information; strategic information from website activity, that can be used to better meet the needs of e-customers and to sell more products.

(3) Metrics are needed to provide accountability and to analyze the information for strategic advantage.

Preparing the E-Marketing Plan

S. Writing an e-marketing plan is not an easy task. There are obstacles. However, the intent of this unit is not to provide a guide for developing an e-marketing plan, rather, we will identify some of the hurdles that must be overcome to develop a good plan.

T. For starters, procrastination is a problem; busy executives will put off writing a plan. Yet, with businesses moving at such a rapid pace (Internet time), there is a big opportunity cost to e-procrastination. Putting off the development of an e-marketing plan can cost you market opportunities and profits.

U. Another obstacle is time. The process of developing an e-marketing plan is time-consuming. Think about ways to streamline the process. Examples and templates could be the answer. Seeing an example plan to emulate and following a proven template can save you a great deal of time. A template suggests an effective outline, headings, and in some cases, texts.

V. Other issues related to the writing process such as writer's block and the labor-intensive circuitous nature of writing are also major barriers. Other difficulties include the challenge of identifying the right analysis, the tricky nature of developing revenue stream forecasts, and question of which expense budgets to develop.

Words and Expressions

benchmark ['bentʃmɑːk]	n.	基准，衡量尺度
inbound ['ɪnbaʊnd]	adj.	归航的，入站的
incur [ɪn'kɜː(r)]	v.	招致，带来
portal ['pɔːtl]	n.	门户（网站），正文
populate ['pɒpjuleɪt]	v.	居住于，栖居于
premium ['priːmiəm]	n.	额外费用，保险费
hurdle ['hɜːdl]	n.	障碍，跨栏赛跑
procrastination [prəʊˌkræstɪ'neɪʃ(ə)n]	n.	延迟，拖延
template ['templeɪt]	n.	样板，模板
emulate ['emjuleɪt]	v.	仿效，模仿
circuitous [sə'kjuːɪtəs]	adj.	迂回的，绕行的

Questions

Directions: In this section, you are required to answer the following questions according to the information in the text.

(1) What is the difference between a marketing plan and an e-marketing plan?

(2) What does a company have to think about when developing an e-marketing plan?

(3) What are benefits of the merchant model?

(4) What are the essential problems to the models identified in the passage?

(5) What are the obstacles of writing a good e-marketing plan?

Exercises

Directions: In this section, you are required to answer the questions with T or F.
T (for True) if the statement agrees with the information given in the passage;
F (for False) if the statement contradicts the information given in the passage.

(1) Some models offer free content with premium content available only to paid subscribers. Advertising revenues may also be part of the revenue stream.

(2) Revenue streams are derived from licensing of the auction technology platform, transaction fees, and advertising.

(3) Virtual communities model ranges from virtual malls to online stock and bond traders and can include business-to-business, business-to-consumer and consumer-to-consumer.

(4) Dell Computer Corporation, maker of personal computer systems is the example of selling direct to consumers via their website.

(5) A business that utilizes the Internet to help other businesses manage logistical functions such as electronic payments, ordering systems, and shipping services in operating under the logistics model.

(6) Through adverting, merchants can place their advertising banners and links on content sites worldwide and only pay a commission when those links generate a sale or a qualified lead.

(7) As you prepare your e-marketing plan, you may go through a learning process; you will analyze your e-business model in detail in an attempt to learn what drives your offline sales and revenue streams.

(8) Virtual communities model makes it easy for the community members to add their own content to the online community website.

(9) The auction includes catalogers who have decided to complement their catalog operation with a website or have decided to migrate completely to an online model.

(10) Unlike a traditional broadcaster or news media business models, the web advertising model provides content and services supported by banner advertisements and other forms of online advertising.

Translation

什么是电子市场营销计划

让我们从定义市场营销计划开始,然后再确定它的"新经济伙伴"——电子营销计划。市场营销计划是一份书面文件,详细记录了当前的销售形势、威胁和机会、营销目标和实现目标的战略。我们既可以给单个的产品、服务、品牌制订市场营销计划,也可以针对公司整体制订一个相应的计划。与传统的市场营销计划相比,电子市场营销计划目标更加明确。虽然它经常包含一些与传统市场营销计划相同的主题,但它更侧重于在互联网上的营销机会、营销威胁、营销目标和营销策略。

电子市场营销计划要定义你的商务模式,从参与执行计划的所有人的角度建立起承诺,并制定业绩标准和成功度量。电子市场营销计划的制订开始于对电子商务模式的全面回顾。什么是电子商务模式呢?本文在接下来的部分里对电子商务模式做了描述。回顾那些描述并思考一下哪一个模式最接近你的电子商务模式。在你开始制订一个电子市场营销计划之前,要考虑怎样来定义你的电子商务模式以及它是怎样影响你的电子市场营销计划的。

电子市场营销计划和电子商务模式

电子市场营销计划为你的电子商务的成功提供了一张路线图或蓝图。写好电子市场营销计划的先决条件是你要对自己的电子商务模式有一个全面彻底的理解。当你准备做电子市场营销计划时,你可能要经历一个学习的过程:你将详细分析你的电子商务模式以了解是什么在驱动着你的在线销售和收益流。

你的电子商务模式是什么?你能否用一两段文字来描述它?业务模型描述了产品、服务和信息交付的架构以及收益来源(收益流)。它描述了企业价值链的基本元素,比如内向物流、操作(或生产)、外向物流、营销、服务以及支持活动。

你必须通过描述你的商务模式来定义它。从描述中,你能识别出每条重要的收益来源和潜在的收益来源吗?你能判断出产生这些收益流所需的费用吗?你知道哪些关键事情(指标)极为重要,必须衡量并跟踪以确保成功吗?你能了解你的商务模式将怎样使用电子市场营销来定价、促销、销售和分销你的产品吗?

当你制订电子市场营销计划时，必须考虑该怎样使你的电子市场营销行为"适合"你的商务模式。至少你的商务模式将影响你对销售额以及电子市场营销费用的预测方式。但是，除了基本的销售预测和预算外，你的电子市场营销计划还应包括你开展业务、产生收益和消耗资源的具体方式等方面的内容。你的电子市场营销计划应该讨论你将如何使用信息技术管理营销组合（产品、价格、渠道和促销），你要如何优化你的内容，以及你将如何分配资源来吸引新的客户，建立已有客户的忠诚度，并创造收益流。

确保在制订计划前明确你的商务模式。你能在下面的描述部分确定你的电子商务模式吗？

经销商模式

经销商模式是商品和服务的批发商或零售商的网络销售。网络上的商品和服务可能是独特的，也可能是传统的"实体店门面"的商品拓展。这种模式包括那些已经决定用一个网站来补充他们的邮购目录销售或者决定完全转换为在线模式的目录营销员。这种模式的优点包括通过进入全球市场来增加对产品和服务的需求、降低销售成本和促销成本的可能性、每天24小时/每周7天的全天候订购和客户服务，以及一对一的客户营销。

拍卖模式

拍卖模式是通过商品和服务的多媒体展示来实现将投标机制引入网络。收益流来自拍卖技术平台的授权许可、交易费和广告。

制造商模式

制造商模式使用网络来压缩分销渠道。它不是通过中介机构把产品和服务推向市场，而是通过网络使其直接到达消费者。例如，个人电脑系统制造商——戴尔公司采用的就是这种模式，他们通过网站直接向消费者销售产品。戴尔公司的销售额的大约50%是通过网站实现的。

关联模式

关联模式是"按业绩支付报酬模式"。当客户点击网页上的链接或者横幅广告来购买商品和服务时，就创造了收益流。关联销售是一个网站（联盟）促成了另一个网站的商品或服务销售（经销商）时就获得佣金。当经销商从一个联盟（合作网站）获得一次销售时，会员提取佣金（如销售额的10%）。通过关联销售，经销商可以将他们的横幅广告和链接放在全球的内容网站上，并且只有在那些链接产生了销售或发现合格的潜在客户时才支付佣金。通过那些能产生收入的链接，关联内容网站可以实现从在线内容向电子商务的转变。

广告模式

像传统的广播公司或新闻媒介商务模式一样，网络广告模式提供由横幅广告和其他在线广告形式（特别是电子邮件新闻组广告）支持的内容和服务（如电子邮件、聊天、论坛、拍卖等）。一些广告模式被称为门户（如美国在线、雅虎和AltaVista），其他的被称为"免费模式"。

信息媒介模式

这是一种依靠从用户那里收集信息并把这些信息销售给其他企业来获利的网络模式。流量主要靠免费服务（比如免费的互联网接入或者免费硬件），来引导到信息媒介网站。

订阅模式

在订阅模式内，用户要为他们访问站点和浏览高价值的内容付费。有时也把免费内容随同付费内容一起提供给付费订阅者。广告收入同样是收益流的一部分。

经纪模式

经纪模式是把买方与卖方集合在一起的一个网络市场制造者。这种模式的范围从虚拟商业区到在线股票和债券商，它包括企业面向企业（B2B）、企业面向消费者（B2C），以及消费者面向消费者（C2C）三种形式。在这个模式下收入来自交易费或者佣金。

虚拟社区模式

虚拟社区模式促进了社区用户（会员、客户、伙伴、学生等）之间的在线互动。这种模式方便了社区成员在社区网站上添加自己的内容。收益流产生于会员费和广告费。

物流模式

在物流模式里，一个企业利用互联网帮助其他企业管理物流功能，例如电子支付、订单系统和运输服务。相关服务费用是收益计划的基础。

电子商务模式和电子市场营销计划

电子商务模式和电子市场营销之间的关系是什么？前面提到的所有模式中的核心问题有以下三个：

（1）为了使得这些模式有效，电子市场营销计划至关重要。

（2）这些模式产生大量的信息；来自网站活动的战略信息，可以用来更好地满足电子客户的需求和出售更多的商品。

（3）需要通过指标度量来提供可信度，并进行信息分析以获得战略优势。

电子市场营销计划的准备

编写电子市场营销计划不是一项容易的任务，其中有不少障碍。本单元的目的不是为制订电子市场营销计划提供指南，而是要指出制订一个好计划所必须克服的困难。

对新手来说，拖延是一个障碍；公务繁忙的经理人会推迟编写计划。然而，随着商业的快速发展（互联网时代），拖延会导致机会成本增加。推迟制订一个电子市场营销计划的代价是市场机会和利润的损失。

另一个障碍是时间。制订一个电子市场营销计划的过程是很费时的。我们应想办法使流程流畅。通过例子和模板我们可以得到解答，即通过模仿一个计划的范例和使用一个经过验证的模板能节省大量的时间。模板可以给出有效的大纲、标题，在有些情况下还可以给出文本。

其他障碍是与编写过程有关的，例如作者创作时的思路阻滞和写作时的反复修改。其他困难包括识别正确分析的挑战、开发收益流预测的复杂性，以及制定哪些费用预算的问题。

Unit 6
Customer Differentiation and Lifecycle Management of E-Marketing

In the world of e-marketing, success is defined by your ability to build long-term customer relationships that bring value to your customer and sustain profitability to your organization.

Technology alone cannot provide a magic solution that will immediately resolve all your marketing challenges. Worldwide, companies are finding e-marketing success by investing in a combination of innovative implementations of technology, business process enhancements, and organizational structure changes that are part of an overall e-marketing strategy.

Customer Differentiation

The first step toward building successful customer relationships begins by adopting a corporate culture that recognizes that every customer is different. Your customers have different interests, different levels of disposable income, different perceptions of value and perhaps most importantly, different historical experiences with your company.

The world of one-size-fits-all mass marketing fails to recognize these differences and use them for competitive advantage. The more you can evangelize a customer-centric corporate culture, revising technology, business processes and organizational structure around recognition of customer differences, the more effective your relationship building strategies will be.

This does not mean that you need to develop a separate plan for each individual customer; rather it challenges you to identify the relative value of customers and create a strategy that effectively targets collective customer needs—starting with your most profitable customers.

Using customer differentiation for e-marketing requires that you not only to identify who your customers are, but more importantly to recognize who are or are likely to become your best customers. You need to develop profiles based on the characteristics of your best customers and use them as the basis for understanding the profile of customers that you want to acquire. Additionally, it is important to recognize differences in profiles based on where the customer is within the customer lifecycle. This will provide you with insight into customer behavior and allow you to address customer needs most effectively.

The metrics you use to define customer value will vary considerably based on the types of customers you have and your goals. A few key value indicators you may want to consider include:

(1) Transaction history.

(2) Profitability.

(3) Length of the customer relationship.

(4) Cost to service.

To ensure that your value indicators continue to provide valid measurement over time, you'll need to regularly reassess the components that define customer value.

Customer Lifecycle Management

Customer lifecycle is another key e-marketing factor you must address to successfully build customer relationships. While marketers have traditionally used a variety of terms to define the stages of the customer lifecycle, for the purposes of this document we'll use acquire, engage, extend, and retain.

As we focus on strategies for building relationships across phases of the customer lifecycle, our emphasis will be on the business benefits of these strategies. Fundamental to the assumption of business benefit is that the strategy also delivers value to the customer. Like personal relationships, business relationships are best when built on mutual respect, trust, and value to all parties involved.

Acquire

Recent studies show a decrease in the cost to acquire new online customers. However, this doesn't mean your acquisition efforts don't need a well thought out plan and approach. Some of the basic elements that make your site appealing to new customers are detailed below.

(1) Registration Incentives: Contests, promotions, white papers product samples, and demos are all examples of incentives you can provide to get new customers to register or purchase products or services. Customers need to have a clear value proposition in order to be willing to

disclose information and begin a relationship with you. Develop a plan to entice customers to come to your site, and track the effectiveness of the promotions and other incentives. Prominently display incentives on your site—so much the better if these incentives are tightly bound to relevant services.

(2) Referral Incentives: Giving incentive to current customers to refer new customers can be a cost-effective way to generate new business. Existing customers are happy to refer others, provided they are happy with the products or services they are receiving and see value in the incentive provided.

(3) Easy Navigation and Robust Search Capability: To get customers to your site, make sure your basic design is planned with your customers in mind. Some of the basic requirements to consider include:

① A visually appealing user interface with a clear message.

② Straightforward navigation on the site; users should never get stranded or lost on your site.

③ Robust, easy-to-use search capabilities.

(4) Brand Establishment and Messaging: New brands need development of messages and advertisements to convey their identity to customers. Make sure that the online experience for existing brands with well-known messages is consistent and leverages the same message as their offline advertising and messaging.

Engage

Use content or services to ensure a positive initial experience with your company. Engage visitors in an interactive dialog that goes beyond the initial interest or sale. Demonstrate your knowledge of the product offering as a way to distinguish yourself from your competitors. Welcome visitors to the community. Make it easy for them to do business with you. Provide engaging features that will keep them coming back, as follows.

(1) Content: The most fundamentally engaging feature is simply a web resource that always has something new to offer when the visitor returns. Ever-changing content, like window-dressing in a storefront, provides a compelling reason for customers to return to your site. This may seem basic, but too few enterprises accurately forecast the staffing and organization needed to sustain lively content over time.

(2) Community Features: Community features such as discussion boards, feedback mechanisms, webcasts, and live chats are proven methods for bringing visitors back to your site. These features actually involve visitors in creating much of your ever-changing content.

(3) Pre-populate Data: To simplify the ordering process, eliminate redundant data collection by pre-populating information. Pre-populating data based on past visits or information entered

during the session can expedite the ordering process and make it easier for your customers to use your site. Customers appreciate ease of use and will be more inclined to return to order again.

(4) Notifications, Recommendations, and Alerts Based on Customer Preferences: Provide the ability to customize communications to your customers. Provide notice of promotions and news alerts based on user-indicated preferences.

(5) Online Product Configuration: Provide your customers with the ability to configure your products and services online. Give your customers the information they need to be able to configure products based on their specific requirements.

Extend

When you have truly engaged your customers and established the foundation of a relationship, it is time to look at ways to extend that relationship. Uncovering opportunities to provide additional value-added products and services when built on a solid relationship will not only benefit the customer, but will also enhance the lifetime value of the customer.

(1) Auto Replenishment: Develop a plan to auto-replenish products ordered by your top customers.

(2) Personalized Recommendations: Use data mining and analysis of purchase and transaction history to identify personalized recommendations including potential cross-sell and up-sell opportunities. Intelligently suggesting related products or product upgrades is not only a valuable service to customers, but also a successful method of extending your customer share both vertically and horizontally. Develop targeted campaigns to promote cross-sell and up-sell products and services.

(3) Lifetime Event Selling: Based on the information you have from customers, anticipate lifetime events and develop promotions to make customers aware of products and services you provide based on the event. Examples include promoting PC's when customer's children reach school age, or promoting travel packages for active retirees.

(4) Partner to Complement Your Offering: Develop partnerships and affiliations with other organizations that allow you to provide a complete and compelling package for your customers.

Retain

Retaining customers requires an ongoing commitment to provide increasing levels of value to the customer. Enhancing retention requires customers to continue to provide information about themselves, through their responses and their behavior, so that you are better able to target products and services. Additionally, if your established services make it significantly easier for customers to do businesses with your organization compared to your competitors, these services provide barriers to attrition.

Unit 6 Customer Differentiation and Lifecycle Management of E-Marketing

(1) Customer-defined Experience: Provide the ability for your customers to customize the content they receive and when and how they receive it when visiting your site. Letting the customer define the experience as much as possible lets the customer know you are in business to serve them. By defining their experience with the information they want, the customer is providing you with valuable information about their needs. Additionally, they are indicating a willingness to do business with you and provide more information about themselves and their interests.

(2) Differentiate Service Programs: Provide higher levels of service for customers that you have designated as your best customers.

(3) Loyalty and Reward Programs: Develop specific programs that reward your customers for making purchases and that encourage them to continue to purchase from your site. Loyalty programs can vary from simple to complex depending upon the products and services you offer.

Words and Expressions

evangelize [ɪ'vændʒəlaɪz]	v.	使皈依，向……传教
entice [ɪn'taɪs]	v.	诱惑，诱使
referral [rɪ'fɜːrəl]	n.	移交；送交
strand [strænd]	v.	使滞留，使搁浅
leverage ['liːvərɪdʒ]	v.	利用，举债经营
redundant [rɪ'dʌndənt]	adj.	多余的，过剩的
expedite ['ekspədaɪt]	v.	使加速完成，促进
configuration [kənˌfɪɡə'reɪʃn]	n.	布局，配置
replenishment [rɪ'plenɪʃmənt]	n.	补充，重新装满
attrition [ə'trɪʃn]	n.	损耗，人员缩减

Questions

Directions: In this section, you are required to answer the following questions according to the information in the text.

(1) What are the requirements for using customer differentiation for e-marketing purposes?

(2) What are the essential indicators to judge customer value?

(3) What should be taken into account when a company plans its design to get the customer to its site?

(4) What does a company need to do in order to keep loyal customers?

(5) Which stage of the customer lifecycle do you think is most important in establishing a successful customer relationship, and why?

Exercises

Directions: In this section, there are five questions and for each of them there are four choices marked A, B, C and D. You should decide on the best choice.

(1) What does an overall e-marketing strategy not include according to the passage?

    A. Business process enhancements.

    B. Innovative implementations of technology.

    C. Competitive advantages.

    D. Organizational changes.

(2) What should be emphasized when focusing on strategies for building relationships across phases of the customer lifecycle?

    A. The changes of these strategies.

    B. The implementations of these strategies.

    C. The development of these strategies.

    D. The business benefits of these strategies.

(3) When will existing customers be glad to refer others to your company?

    A. They have a clear value proposition to begin a relationship with you.

    B. They are satisfied with the products or services they are receiving.

    C. They have different historical experiences with your company.

    D. They want to get much incentives from your company.

(4) What is ignored by most enterprises according to the passage?

    A. Sustaining lively content over time.

    B. Competing with other rivals.

    C. Communicating with customers.

    D. Promoting their products.

(5) What is the successful way of extending your customer share both vertically and horizontally?

    A. Frequently promoting PC's when customer's children reach school age.

    B. Intelligently suggesting related products or product upgrades.

    C. Actively uncovering opportunities to provide additional value-added products.

    D. Directly developing plans to auto-replenish products ordered by customers.

Unit 6　Customer Differentiation and Lifecycle Management of E-Marketing

Translation

电子市场营销的客户差异化与生命周期管理

在电子市场营销世界中，企业的成功与否取决于其与客户构建长期的客户关系的能力，这种长期的客户关系在给客户带来价值的同时，也能够让你的组织拥有持续的获利能力。

仅仅依靠技术无法给企业提供一把能够即刻解决企业面临的各种营销挑战的万能钥匙。在世界范围内，许多企业都致力于组合运用多种手段来探索电子营销的成功之道，包括技术创新应用、业务流程优化以及作为整体电子营销策略的重要组成部分的组织结构变革。

客户差异化

建立成功客户关系的第一步便是要构建起一种以"每一位客户都各不相同"为理念的企业文化。你的客户不但具有不同的兴趣爱好、不同的可支配收入、不同的价值观，可能还有最重要的一点就是他们过去与你的企业打交道的感受各有差异。

那些一直以一种模式满足所有客户需求进行大规模营销的企业显然未能认识到这些差异，更未能利用这些差异形成独特的竞争优势。你越是坚持以客户为中心的企业文化，越是根据客户的不同需求来改进技术、业务流程以及组织结构，你的客户关系建立策略就越有效。

但这并不意味着你需要为每一位客户量身定做出不同的计划，而需要面对的挑战是：你必须能识别出客户的相对价值，并从最具利润价值的客户入手，制定出一个有效的、以满足群体客户需求为目标的战略。

把客户差异化应用于电子营销，不仅要求你能识别出谁是你的客户，更重要的是让你能确认谁已经是你的最佳客户或谁极可能成为你的最佳客户。你应该分析并总结出现有的最佳客户的"画像"，对照这些，再来理解你希望争取的客户的特征。此外，根据客户所处的生命周期的位置来识别客户特征的差异也是非常重要的，这样做可以帮助你更好地洞察客户行为，并且最有效地处理客户的需求。

客户的类型各异，企业目标不同，定义客户价值的标准也会有很大的变化。你应该考虑的一些关键价值指标包括：

（1）交易历史。

（2）获利能力。

（3）客户关系维持时间的长短。

（4）服务成本。

为了确保你所使用的价值指标能够持续提供准确而有效的评估，你需要定期对这些定义客户价值的要素进行重新评价。

客户生命周期管理

客户生命周期是你在成功构建客户关系时必须处理好的另一个关键性的电子营销要素。从传统上来看，市场研究人员曾使用各种各样的术语来定义客户生命周期的各个阶段，但出于本文的目的，我们将其划分为获取客户信息、吸引客户注意、扩展客户和留住客户四个阶段。

当我们关注在客户生命周期的不同阶段，为了建立有效的客户关系应采取的战略时，我们的重点将是这些战略所能带来的商业价值。商业价值假设的基础是这一战略也能给客户带来价值。同人际关系一样，商业关系也是建立在相互尊重、信任以及对每一个参与者都有利的基础上的。

获取客户信息

最近的研究表明，获得新的在线客户的成本正在不断降低，但这并不意味着"获取客户"阶段不需要一个考虑周详的计划和方法。下面详细介绍一些使网站能吸引新客户的基本要素。

（1）注册激励：竞赛、促销活动、白皮书产品样本以及试销产品都是吸引新客户注册或购买产品或服务的有效手段。客户只有在一个明确的价值取向的引导下，才愿意公开自己的信息并与你建立客户关系。因此，企业需要制订一个计划来吸引客户访问自己的网站，并跟踪其促销和其他激励的实施效果。将激励元素放在网站显著的位置——如果这些激励元素与相关的服务紧密联系起来，效果将会更好。

（2）推荐激励：激励现有客户介绍新的客户可能是创造新业务的一种具有成本效益的方式。如果现有客户对公司所提供的产品或者服务感到满意，而且可以从所提供的激励因素中获得利益，那么他们将很愿意把别人介绍进来。

（3）易于浏览和强大的搜索功能：为了吸引更多的客户登录，必须牢记网站设计的基本出发点是为客户着想的。一些需要考虑的基本要求包括：

① 一个提供清晰信息，且视觉上富有吸引力的用户界面。

② 简单明了的导航；使用者不应该感到束手无策或迷失方向。

③ 强大的、易于使用的搜索功能。

Unit 6　Customer Differentiation and Lifecycle Management of E-Marketing

（4）品牌建立与广告宣传：新的品牌需要开发相应的广告词并做广告宣传，才能向客户传达品牌特征。要确保那些有很高知名度的品牌的在线体验是一致的，以及利用与他们的线下相同的广告及信息。

吸引客户注意

要利用相应的内容或服务以确保客户对你的公司留下积极的初步印象。促进网站访问者与企业的交互对话，以超越最初的利润或销售。向你的客户展示你对所提供的产品的了解，以使你与其他竞争者更好地区分开来。欢迎访问者进入讨论社区。让客户与公司更加轻松地做生意。另外还应在网站上提供如下特色服务来吸引客户的回访。

（1）内容：最基本的吸引客户的手段就是在网站资源上做文章，当客户回访时，能够看到新的内容。不断变化的内容，就像沿街店面的橱窗布置一样，总能给人耳目一新的感觉，这就为客户提供了一个回访网站的充足理由。这看起来是基本要求，但很少有企业能够准确预测为了长期输出生动的内容所需要的人员配置和组织设置的情况。

（2）社区特色：社区特色，如讨论区、反馈机制、网络广播和在线聊天被证明是有效吸引客户回访的方法。社区特色实际上让访问者参与创建许多不断更新的网站内容。

（3）直接载入数据：为了简化订购流程，可以使用直接载入数据的功能来减少冗余信息的收集。直接载入的数据来源于客户先前的访问以及在交易期间客户提供的数据。此项功能可以加快订购流程并使得网站更容易使用。客户将因为网站易于使用而再次访问并订购商品。

（4）基于客户偏好的提示、建议和警报：向客户提供能够实现个性化沟通的能力。根据客户指示的偏好提供促销信息和新闻告示。

（5）在线产品配置：拥有为客户提供在线配置产品和服务的能力，并向客户提供相关的信息，以使他们可以依据自己的特殊需求自由配置各类产品。

扩展客户

在你已经真正地同你的客户建立起了客户关系后，接下来要做的就是扩展这种客户关系。寻找机会为客户提供增值产品或者额外的服务，不仅仅会使客户受益，而且可以提高客户的终身价值。

（1）自动补货：制订计划，自动补充高端客户订购的产品。

（2）个性化推荐：使用数据挖掘的方法对以往客户采购和交易的历史数据进行深度分析，以确认个性化推荐，如潜在的交叉销售和追加销售的机会。向客户智能地推荐相关产品或者是升级产品，不但为客户提供了有价值的服务，而且还实现了你的客户份额的横向和纵向的扩展。有针对性地开展促销活动，以促进产品和服务的交叉营销或者追加销售。

（3）客户人生事件营销：依据你获得的客户信息，预测客户的人生事件，制订促销计划，让客户意识到你的产品和服务是根据这些事件提供的，如当客户的孩子到了上学年龄时，就可以向客户推销个人电脑，或向活跃的退休人员推销旅游套餐。

（4）能够填补产品空白的合作伙伴：同其他企业发展伙伴和附属关系，让你为你的客户提供完整的、不可抗拒的商品。

留住客户

为了留住客户，企业需要能够长期持续不断地向客户提供日益提高的价值水平。提高客户的留存率，需要客户能不断地向企业提供他们自己的信息，通过他们的反应和行为，只有这样，你才能更好地定位产品或服务。此外，如果和竞争对手相比，你的服务能让客户和你进行交易更容易，那么这些服务就会减少客户流失。

（1）客户自定义的体验：当客户访问你的网站时，应为他们提供这样的能力，即能够让他们自主确定自己所需要的内容，并由他们自己确定何时以及如何获得内容。尽量让客户自己来定义体验，让客户察觉到你正在为他们提供服务。如果让客户按他们需要的信息来定义自己的体验，那么客户就会向你提供更多有价值的有关他们需求的信息。此外，客户也会表示愿意与你开展业务，并能提供更多的关于他们自己及其兴趣的信息给你。

（2）差异化服务计划：为那些已经被你认定为最佳客户的客户提供更高水平的服务。

（3）忠诚以及奖励计划：制订特定的计划以奖励已经购买产品的客户，并鼓励他们继续通过你的网站来购买产品或者服务。可以依据你所提供的产品或服务的差异而具体制订繁简不一的客户忠诚计划。

Chapter 3　E-Business about Enterprises
第 3 篇　企业电子商务

- **UNIT 7**　Challenges of Establishing Online Business in the E-Commerce Process Chain

- **UNIT 8**　How SMBs Can Profit from the Internet

- **UNIT 9**　Could My Business Be an E-Business

UNIT 7 Challenges of Establishing Online Business in the E-Commerce Process Chain

A. The first step for companies to engage in e-commerce is to establish an online presence, which could be through a virtual shop or an e-commerce platform, or adding an e-commerce module on a company's website. A set of questions in the survey were focused on identifying what micro, small and medium-sized enterprises (MSMEs) find to be the most challenging issues when they establish an online business (see Table 7.1). It appears that the most frequently reported challenges are a lack of online visibility from potential customers from other countries (accounting for 27% in overall reported challenges), a lack of technical skills (21%), and the high cost of membership fees in e-commerce platforms (15%). Below are the main takeaway messages for the survey findings related to establishing online business.

Table 7.1 Bottleneck analysis in establishing an online business

Chanllenges	Percentages
Online visibility	27%
Technical skills	21%
Cost of membership fees in platforms	15%
Business knowledges	9%
Platforms requirements	9%
Languages skills	7%
Platform access as merchant	6%
Internet access	3%
Others	3%

Note: The percentages represent the respective weight in the overall set of challenges.

Online visibility: A greater challenge than Internet access

B. Contrary to the perception that Internet infrastructure is a major bottleneck for developing countries and LDCs, only a small number of respondents (3%) reported that lack of reliable Internet access is a challenge to establish their online business, and there is no visible gap for developing and African country respondents. This could signal that the Internet infrastructure in developing countries has been improving in recent years, but it might also be due to the way the survey was conducted. As it was an open online survey, responses were mainly from those who already have Internet access. The far more prominent challenge highlighted by the majority of respondents was the lack of visibility from potential customers (27% of overall challenges). Online shops do not automatically attract customers. Even with a fully functional online shop, companies still need to invest substantially in online and offline marketing to draw business to their online operations.

C. This finding is further supported by many companies' supplementary comments that indicated that even when they had already established an online shop, it generated little, or in many cases zero, transactions. To improve online visibility, some respondents emphasized the need to master online marketing tools and gain better knowledge about potential markets and platforms.

For certain products such as agricultural products and handicrafts, specialized online distribution channels might be better than general e-commerce platforms.

D. Investing in improving online visibility often implies substantial financial commitment. However, MSMEs find it challenging to commit already limited financial resources into online marketing without knowing the return and success rate of such investments. Access to finance is also a challenge for MSMEs who want to expand their online business, as highlighted by a cooperative of 45 farmers who suggested that there should be financial support for online promotion, such as marketing through AdWords.

Technical skills and business knowledge: Key challenges in establishing online businesses

E. Technical skills required to set up online operations may include coding, editing images, providing accurate product description and navigating e-commerce platform memberships. Business knowledge refers to the ability to analyze the business success of e-commerce operations, including understanding market demand and defining growth strategies.

F. Respondents ranked lack of technical skills and business knowledge second and fourth in all reported challenges, accounting for 21% and 9% respectively. In addition to coding and image processing skills, some respondents also said they lacked other technical

Unit 7 Challenges of Establishing Online Business in the E-Commerce Process Chain

skills specific to e-commerce, such as maintaining and managing a reliable stock system, and using international article numbers for their products, which are required by some e-commerce platforms.

G. For business knowledge, the common challenges among respondents were a lack of market information and understanding of successful business models for e-commerce. While the majority see e-commerce as a channel for distribution, some companies also use it as a way of gathering market information. For instance, some firms reported they open accounts on online platforms mainly for the sake of collecting price information in different markets, and testing demand for their products in foreign markets. Some respondents also mentioned they do not know how to trade internationally, often lacking familiarity with customs procedures, documents and requirements.

Developing country firms face more challenges

H. Whereas technical skills and business knowledge are related to the establishment phase, when companies attempt to create their online business, lack of online visibility is a major obstacle in the operational phase, when the shop is online and operational. In the survey findings, there is a clear distinction between developed and developing countries in terms of these two phases.

I. Companies from developing countries reported more challenges in the establishment phase. Technical skills and business knowledge combined represented 34% of total challenges for companies from developing countries, versus 26% in developed countries. Language skills were also mentioned as hampering firms' ability to establish an online business for cross-border e-commerce (7%). Companies from developed countries reported more challenges in the operational phase. Online visibility accounted for 24% of total challenges for developing country companies, versus 30% for companies from developed countries. This does not necessarily mean that developing country MSMEs face less challenges in the operational phase, but rather only reflects that they encounter challenges earlier than companies from developed countries.

J. Online visibility in the operational phase is also a knowledge and skill issue. However, compared with the knowledge and skills required for setting up a virtual business, improving online visibility involves much more sophisticated technical skills, such as search engine optimization, and business knowledge to operate in different markets and manage online marketing and promotions.

E-commerce platform access and fees: Greater issues for developing country firms

K. The cost of membership fees in cross-border e-commerce platforms ranked third among all major challenges (15%), and this was a more prominent challenge for companies in

African countries (19%). In addition to, or in place of, membership fees, some e-commerce platforms charge a relatively high commission on the sales conducted through the platforms. Some e-commerce platforms, for example, may charge up to 40% commission on sales. Large international platforms usually charge between 7% and 15% commission. These rates are set depending on the estimated or perceived operational costs and risks, which means that rates are usually higher in developing countries and LDCs.

L. Access to e-commerce platforms is also a more prominent issue for companies from developing countries (9%) and African countries (10%) than developed countries (3%).

M. Respondents highlighted several reasons for being denied access to e-commerce platforms, such as the e-commerce platform does not allow registration by companies from their country; companies were unable to provide proof of formal company registration, trading history, identity of directors or managers of the firm; companies did not have access to an online payment mechanism. Companies from Africa find it more challenging to meet documentation requirements, particularly trading history, and respondents from Africa reported more instances where their shops were closed down following repeated customer complaints.

N. As identified in previous ITC and UNCTAD studies, not all e-commerce platforms offer their services in all countries. For instance, Amazon allows registration as seller from 103 countries. Among the countries not allowed to register, many are LDCs. To register as a seller on Amazon, companies or individuals need to be a resident of one of the 103 countries allowed, have a local phone number and have an internationally chargeable credit card. To obtain an internationally chargeable credit card could already be a challenge for some micro-sized firms operating in LDCs.

O. Interoperability and transferability of data between e-commerce platforms are also reported as challenges for some MSMEs. Companies often cannot freely transfer their data from one e-commerce platform to another, and need to manually recreate their online shops if they want to operate on a new platform. Apart from the additional cost of manually creating a new shop, the greatest challenge is non-transferability of transaction records.

P. Transaction records are a verifiable trace of a company's performance and trustworthiness, which is vitally important for online businesses to attract new consumers or partners. E-commerce platforms typically claim ownership over these transaction records and other transaction-related data, which may imply a high platform-switching cost for MSMEs.

Unit 7 Challenges of Establishing Online Business in the E-Commerce Process Chain

Words and Expressions

infrastructure ['ɪnfrəstrʌktʃə]	n.	基础建设；基础设施
signal ['sɪgnəl]	v.	（用手势、声音等）发信号；示意
prominent ['prɒmɪnənt]	adj.	著名的；突出的
supplementary [ˌsʌplɪ'mentri]	adj.	增补性的，额外的
substantial [səb'stænʃl]	adj.	大量的；结实的
hamper ['hæmpə(r)]	v.	妨碍，束缚
commission [kə'mɪʃn]	n.	佣金，手续费
documentation [ˌdɒkjumen'teɪʃn]	n.	文件证据；文献资料
interoperability ['ɪntərɒpərə'bɪlətɪ]	n.	互用性，协同工作的能力
verifiable ['verɪfaɪəbl]	adj.	可证实的，可核实的

Questions

Directions: In this section, you are required to answer the following questions according to the information in the text.

(1) What is the purpose of the survey?

(2) How can companies improve their online visibility according to some respondents?

(3) What are other problems about technical skills specific to e-commerce for some respondents besides coding and image processing skills?

(4) What is the major difference between developed and developing countries when shops are online and operational?

(5) What is more challenging for African companies?

Exercises

Directions: In this section, you are going to read ten statements attached to the text. Each statement contains information given in one of the paragraphs in the text. Identify the paragraph from which the information is derived. You may choose a paragraph more than once.

(1) According to previous ITC and UNCTAD studies, not all e-commerce platforms offer their services in all countries.

(2) Apart from the additional cost of manually creating a new shop, the greatest challenge is non-transferability of transaction records.

(3) According to the results of the survey, lack of reliable Internet access is not a big challenge to establish their online business, and there is no visible gap for developing and African country respondents.

(4) Some firms reported they open accounts on online platforms mainly for the sake of collecting price information in different markets, and testing demand for their products in foreign markets.

(5) In addition to, or in place of, membership fees, some e-commerce platforms charge a relatively high commission on the sales conducted through the platforms.

(6) While technical skills and business knowledge are related to the establishment phase, when companies attempt to create their online business, lack of online visibility is a major obstacle in the operational phase, when the shop is online and operational.

(7) Despite an online shop with full functions, companies still need to invest substantially in online and offline marketing to draw business to their online operations.

(8) It is difficult for MSMEs to commit already limited financial resources into online marketing without knowing the return and success rate of such investments.

(9) Compared with the knowledge and skills required for setting up a virtual business, improving online visibility involves much more sophisticated technical skills.

(10) Business knowledge refers to the ability to analyze the business success of e-commerce operations, including understanding market demand and defining growth strategies.

Unit 7 Challenges of Establishing Online Business in the E-Commerce Process Chain

Translation

电子商务流程中建立网上业务面临的挑战

企业参与电子商务的第一步是建立在线业务,可以是通过虚拟商店或电子商务平台,也可以是在公司网站上添加电子商务模块。调查中的一系列问题集中在确定微型、小型和中型企业在建立在线业务时遇到的最具挑战性的问题(见表7.1)。最常见的挑战似乎是在其他国家的潜在客户中缺乏在线可见度(占27%),缺乏技术(占21%),电子商务平台的高昂会员费(占15%)。以下是与建立在线业务相关的调查结果的主要结论。

表7.1 最具挑战性的问题

挑战	百分比
在线可见度	27%
技术技能	21%
平台会员费	15%
商务知识	9%
平台需求	9%
语言能力	7%
作为商家的平台接入	6%
互联网接入	3%
其他	3%

注:百分比代表整体挑战中的各自权重。

在线知名度:比互联网接入更大的挑战

与互联网基础设施是发展中国家和最不发达国家的主要瓶颈的看法相反,只有少数受访者(3%)表示,缺乏可靠的互联网接入是建立其在线业务的一个挑战,发展中国家和非洲国家的受访者没有明显的差距。这可能表明近年来发展中国家的互联网基础设施建设有所改善,但也可能是由进行调查的方式所致。由于这是一项公开的在线调查,受访者主要来自那些已经能够上网的人。大多数受访者强调的更为突出的挑战是在潜在客户中缺乏在线可见度(占总体的27%)。网上商店不会自动吸引顾客。即使有了一个功能齐全的在线商店,公司仍然需要大量投资于在线和离线营销,以吸引顾客。

许多公司的补充意见进一步支持了这一结论，这些意见表明，即使它们已经建立了一个在线商店，它产生的业务量也很少，或者许多情况下是零交易。为了提高在线知名度，一些受访者强调企业需要掌握在线营销工具，并更好地了解潜在的市场和平台。

对于某些产品，如农产品和手工艺品，专门的在线分销渠道可能优于一般的电子商务平台。

提高在线知名度方面的投资往往意味着大量的资金投入。然而，中型、小型和微型企业发现，在不知道此类投资的回报率和成功率的情况下，将本已有限的财力投入在线营销是一项挑战。资金获取对希望扩大其在线业务的中型、小型和微型企业来说也是一项挑战。一个由45名农民经营的合作社的例子突出表明了这一点，他们建议为在线推广提供资金支持，比如通过AdWords（谷歌的赞助商链接）进行营销。

技术技能和商务知识：建立在线业务的主要挑战

建立在线业务所需的技术技能可能包括编码、图像处理、提供准确的产品描述和管理电子商务平台成员资格。商务知识是指分析电子商务业务成功的能力，包括了解市场需求和确定增长战略。

在所有的挑战中，受访者将缺乏技术技能和商务知识排在第二位和第四位，分别占21%和9%。除了编码和图像处理技能之外，一些受访者还表示，他们缺乏其他专门用于电子商务的技术技能，比如维护和管理可靠的库存系统，以及为他们的产品使用国际商品编号，这是一些电子商务平台所需要的。

就商务知识而言，受访者面临的共同挑战是缺乏市场信息和对成功电子商务商业模式的理解。虽然大多数人认为电子商务是一种分销渠道，但一些公司也将其作为一种收集市场信息的方式。例如，一些公司报告说，它们在线上平台上开设账户主要是为了在不同市场收集价格信息，并在国外市场测试其产品的需求。一些受访者还提到，他们不知道如何进行国际贸易，通常是因为不熟悉海关程序、文件和要求。

发展中国家企业面临更多挑战

虽然技术技能和商务知识与建立在线业务阶段有关，但在运营阶段，当公司试图创建其在线业务时，缺乏在线知名度是一个主要障碍，因为商店是在线运营的。调查结果显示，发达国家和发展中国家的企业在这两个阶段有着明显的区别。

发展中国家的公司受访者表示，在创建在线业务阶段面临更多的挑战。技术技能和商务知识方面的挑战合计在发展中国家公司中占34%，而在发达国家则占26%。语言技能也被认为是公司建立跨境电子商务在线业务的阻碍（占7%）。发达国家的公司表示，在运营阶段面临更多的挑战。在线知名度的挑战在发展中国家的公司中占24%，而在发达国家的公司中占30%。这并不一定意味着发展中国家的中型、小型和微型企业在运营阶段面临的挑战较少，而只是反映出它们比发达国家的公司更早地遇到挑战。

Unit 7 Challenges of Establishing Online Business in the E-Commerce Process Chain

运营阶段的在线知名度也是一个知识和技能问题。然而，与建立在线企业所需的知识和技能相比，提高在线知名度涉及更复杂的技术技能，如搜索引擎优化以及在不同市场运营和管理在线营销和促销的业务知识。

电子商务平台接入和收费：发展中国家公司面临的更大问题

在所有主要挑战中，跨境电子商务平台的会员费成本排在第三位(15%)，这对非洲国家的公司来说是一个更为突出的挑战(19%)。除了会员费之外，或者是替代了会员费，一些电子商务平台对通过这些平台进行的销售业务收取相对较高的佣金。例如，一些电子商务平台可能收取高达40%的销售佣金。大型国际平台通常收取7%至15%的佣金。这些费率取决于预计的运营成本和风险，这意味着发展中国家和最不发达国家的费率往往更高。

电子商务平台准入对发展中国家（9%）和非洲国家（10%）的公司来说也是一个更为突出的问题，而发达国家则是3%。

受访者强调了被拒绝进入电子商务平台的几个原因，例如：电子商务平台不允许该国公司注册；公司无法提供公司正式注册、交易历史、董事或经理身份的证明；公司无法使用在线支付机制。来自非洲的公司发现满足文件要求，特别是交易历史方面的要求更具挑战性。非洲的受访者列举了多个由于顾客多次投诉商店被关闭的例子。

正如国际贸易中心和联合国贸易与发展会议以前的研究所指出的，并非所有电子商务平台都在所有国家提供服务。例如，亚马逊（Amazon）允许103个国家的卖方注册。在不被允许注册的国家中，有许多是最不发达国家。要在亚马逊（Amazon）注册为卖家，公司或个人必须是被允许的103个国家中的一个国家的居民，拥有一个本地电话号码，并拥有一张可以国际支付的信用卡。对于在不发达国家经营的一些微型公司来说，获得一张可以国际支付的信用卡可能已经是一个挑战。

电子商务平台之间的数据互操作性和可转移性也成为一些中型、小型和微型企业面临的挑战。企业往往不能自由地将数据从一个电子商务平台转移到另一个电子商务平台，如果它们想在一个新平台上运行，则需要手动重新创建它们的在线商店。除了手动创建新商店的额外成本外，最大的挑战是交易记录的不可转移性。

交易记录是一家公司业绩和信誉的可验证痕迹，这对于在线企业吸引新的消费者或合作伙伴至关重要。电子商务平台通常声称对这些交易记录和其他与交易相关的数据拥有所有权，这可能意味着中型、小型和微型企业面临很高的平台转换成本。

UNIT 8
How SMBs Can Profit from the Internet

A. Businesses of every shape and size have moved to the Internet at an unprecedented rate. The majority of small and medium-sized businesses (SMBs) moved from Internet-interested to Internet-active in just three years. Almost all medium-sized firms have access to the Internet, as do about three-quarters of PC-owning small businesses. The share increases to more than 80% once a firm grows to 10 employees or more.

B. Once on the Internet, small businesses appear ready to take the next step and add a web presence; in fact, two out of five have already done so. When it comes to ecommerce, however, adoption has not been as fast, with only about one-third of small businesses with their own URL actually selling online (i.e., taking the order over the Internet or executing over the phone or by mail after the decision to buy was made while online).

C. Online SMBs without a web presence are very interested in taking the next step of promoting themselves actively on the Internet. About one-fifth of online firms expect to develop their own home page in the next 12 months. About one in eight plans to implement an ecommerce solution. Clearly, small businesses have taken the first steps toward e-business by obtaining Internet access.

D. Although most SMBs recognize the opportunity in doing more through the Internet, relatively few have made the investment, either financially or philosophically, to incorporate e-business fully. For even the most "hands-on" small business owner, the commitment necessary to make effective use of new technologies may initially seem overwhelming. They may well ask, "Will the investment pay dividends?"

E. Sales growth is even more dramatically tied to technology investment. While 29.8% of small businesses indicate that their revenue grew by 10% or more in the past 12 months, 37.9%

of small firms with a web presence report this level of revenue growth. Not surprisingly, more and more SMBs are asking the question: What's the best way to capitalize on the opportunities represented by the Internet?

F. IDC recommends that SMBs stepping up to e-business should think of a four-stage process, with inward- or employee-facing components and outward- or customer- / partner-facing ones that provide escalating benefits with each new stage.

G. Stage 1: Foundation strategy. The process begins with establishing broadband Internet access. Connecting to the Internet with a permanent, broadband link requires a modest investment in equipment and services, or you can easily outsource to an Internet service provider (ISP). What are the benefits? Employees can more readily gather information on customers, partners, and competitors, and communicate with customers via e-mail. The connection also serves as the foundation for future e-business steps.

H. Stages 2 and 3: Customer-facing strategy. For the customer-facing process, the second stage involves creating a basic web presence. The third stage calls for providing new, interactive, and personalized services, such as online customer service, order tracking, reservations, product enhancements and promotions, and commerce for customers and partners.

I. Building a basic website with company and product information requires an additional modest investment in web server, catalog software, and content creation and design services. The payback comes from being able to reach customers beyond the local area and providing customers with easy access to such information as products offered. The website also creates the foundation for Stage 3, the delivery of customer services.

J. Delivering interactive and personalized services via the web requires investment in database, customer relationship management (CRM), and ecommerce software, as well as in network and server solutions to ensure reliability and redundancy. Benefits include reduced cost of sales and customer service, the ability to handle customer requests on a 7×24 basis, and the forging of closer bonds with customers and partners.

K. Stages 2 and 3: Employee-facing strategy. For the employee-facing process, the second stage involves creating a corporate intranet, while the third stage calls for developing and deploying enhanced web-based tools for specific organizations, such as sales, customer service, procurement, and finance.

L. With a corporate intranet, SMBs can deliver benefits and product and business information to employees through an internal web portal, eliminating the need for printing and ensuring timely and consistent dissemination of company information at reduced cost. The intranet also provides a more cost-effective way to communicate with remote and mobile employees.

M. Developing and deploying internal transactional applications encourages greater cross-company collaboration. It also reduces the design, deployment, and training costs for new applications and allows the company to bring new products to market faster and more effectively. Employees feel empowered because they have better tools and more information to handle customer requests.

N. Stage 4: Full e-business implementation. The fourth and final stage closes the loop on the customer- and employee-facing processes by interconnecting the SMBS and partners' websites to enable the delivery of a broad array of services, including one-stop shopping, financing, and design services. SMBs benefit by leveraging their partners' sites as new channels for delivering products and services, while customers benefit from the additional value-added services that become available. In addition, leveraging partners' sites allows SMBs to concentrate their investments in core areas of business.

Matching E-Business with Your Goals

O. Efficiently selling, buying, and accessing resources are critical processes that lie at the heart of SMBs' daily business efforts and remain fundamental to long-term success. E-business can serve as an integral and powerful engine to drive these ongoing efforts. However, like all core business improvements, this integration cannot always be achieved instantly. The process needs to be orderly, with incremental changes that are followed through to completion.

P. For most SMBs, undertaking limited, clearly defined e-business initiatives, tied to specific business drivers and highest-benefit opportunities, will be more successful and will provide quicker, more tangible results. Stepping up to e-business generally doesn't require comprehensive reengineering that may take a while to deliver a bottom-line payoff.

Q. As with most business investments, SMBs' goals for technology investment begin with the most basic: meeting fundamental financial objectives. SMBs, regardless of exact size or industry, are remarkably consistent in identifying the most important challenges they must overcome in order to succeed.

R. IDC asked firms what major issues or concerns they view as the most important—in effect, what were the things they worried most about, or what kept them up at night. Customer and staff concerns were consistently cited most frequently by firms in every size category.

S. Not surprisingly, reaching new customers and working more effectively with current ones are considered crucial issues, as are internal issues, such as attracting and retaining qualified staff.

Unit 8　How SMBs Can Profit from the Internet

T. E-business can deliver more effective operations, both externally and internally, by putting simple but powerful technology and tools behind your core business processes. Externally, e-business solutions help SMBs to meet and exceed customer needs more readily and cost-effectively; internally, e-business solutions help to build staff satisfaction and improve employee skills and productivity.

U. Significantly, the benefits of technology, rather than the technology itself, are of interest to SMBs. That's why e-business holds such potential for SMBs competitive advantage in helping improve customer reach and service while enhancing staff effectiveness and satisfaction.

Words and Expressions

initially [ɪ'nɪʃəli]	adv.	最初，开始
dividend ['dɪvɪdend]	n.	股息，红利
outsource ['aʊtsɔːs]	v.	将……外包，外购
payback ['peɪbæk]	v.	回报，收益
redundancy [rɪ'dʌndənsi]	n.	多余，累赘
dissemination [dɪˌsemɪ'neɪʃn]	n.	传播，宣传
loop [luːp]	n.	圈，环
tangible ['tændʒəbl]	adj.	清晰可见的，明显的

Questions

Directions: In this section, you are required to answer the following questions according to the information in the text.

(1) What is the requirement for building a basic website with company and product information?

(2) What can SMBs benefit from the corporate intranet?

(3) What is the function of developing and deploying internal transactional applications?

(4) What will be more successful and provide quicker, more tangible results for most SMBs?

(5) How can e-business deliver more effective operations, both externally and internally?

Exercises

Directions: In this section, you are required to answer the questions with T or F.
T (for True) if the statement agrees with the information given in the passage;
F (for False) if the statement contradicts the information given in the passage.

(1) Stepping up to e-business generally doesn't require comprehensive reengineering that may take a while to deliver a bottom-line payoff.

(2) For even the most "hands-on" small business owner, the commitment necessary to make effective use of new technologies may initially seem overwhelming.

(3) SMBs, regardless of exact size or industry, are remarkably consistent in identifying the most important challenges they must overcome in order to succeed.

(4) Efficiently selling, buying, and accessing resources are not critical processes that lie at the heart of SMBs' daily business efforts and remain fundamental to long-term success.

(5) SMBs benefit by leveraging their partners' sites as original channels for delivering products and services, while customers benefit from the additional value-added services that become available.

(6) Almost all firms have access to the Internet, as do about three-quarters of PC-owning small businesses.

(7) Significantly, the benefits of technology and the technology itself, are of interest to SMBs.

(8) About one-fourth of online firms expect to develop their own home page in the next 12 months.

(9) When it comes to ecommerce, however, adoption has not been as fast, with only about one-third of small businesses with their own URL actually selling online.

(10) Connecting to the Internet with a permanent, broadband link requires a modest investment in equipment and services, or you can easily outsource to an Internet service provider.

Translation

中小企业如何从互联网中获利

各种规模和形态的企业已经开始以一种前所未有的速度转移至互联网。在仅仅三年的时间里,大部分中小企业已从对互联网感兴趣转变为积极参与。几乎所有的中型企业都接入了互联网,3/4拥有PC机的小型企业也能够访问互联网。一旦企业的员工人数增长到10人或者更多,这一比率就将超过80%。

小型企业一旦接入互联网就准备采取下一步措施并且创建网站;实际上,2/5的企业已经这样做了。但是,当谈及电子商务时,其应用并没有如此迅速,只有约1/3拥有自己的网址(URL)的小型企业能真正地做到在线销售(即在网上接受订购,或在网上做出购买决定后,通过电话或电子邮件实现交易)。

没有网站的在线中小企业非常有兴趣采取下一步措施,即在互联网上积极地宣传自己。约1/5的在线企业期望能够在未来的12个月内开发自己的主页。约1/8的企业计划实施电子商务解决方案。很显然,小型企业已经通过接入互联网向电子商务迈出了第一步。

虽然绝大多数的中小企业意识到通过互联网可以有机会做更多事情,但很少有企业在资金上或理念上作出部署以全面发展电子商务。甚至对大多数已经亲身实践的小企业主而言,为了有效利用新技术所需的投资最初看来也是巨大的。他们可能会问:"这些投资能带来分红吗?"

销售增长和技术投资的联系则更为显著。有29.8%的小企业表明,在过去的12个月中它们的收入增长了10%或更多,与此同时,37.9%的拥有网站的小企业表示有同样的收入增长水平。不足为奇的是,越来越多的中小企业在问这样一个问题:利用互联网所带来的机会的最佳方式是什么?

国际数据公司(IDC)建议正在发展电子商务的中小企业考虑四个阶段的过程,即面向内部的或员工的阶段以及面向外部的或客户/合作伙伴的阶段,其中每一个新的阶段都将带来逐步增长的利润。

阶段1:**基础战略**。该过程始于建立宽带互联网的接入。通过宽带接入与互联网建立永久性连接需要对设备和服务进行不太大的投资,或者你能够很轻松地将其外包给网络服务供应商(ISP)。好处是什么?员工能够更容易地收集关于客户、合作伙伴和竞争对手的信息,并通过电子邮件与客户沟通。这种连接也是未来电子商务实施的基础。

阶段2和阶段3：面向客户的战略。 对于面向客户的过程而言，阶段2涉及创建一个基本的网站。阶段3要求为客户提供新的、交互的和个性化的服务，如在线客户服务、订单跟踪、接受预订、产品升级和促销，以及与客户和合作伙伴的商务往来。

创建一个拥有公司和产品信息的基础网站需要对网络服务器、产品目录软件、内容创建和设计服务进行额外的适度投资。其回报来自能够接触到外地客户，并且客户能够很容易地获取所提供产品的信息。创建网站也是为阶段3提供客户服务打好基础。

通过网络提供交互的和个性化的服务需要对数据库、客户关系管理（CRM）、电子商务软件进行投资，也要对网络和服务器解决方案进行投资，以确保可靠性和冗余度。其好处包括：降低销售成本和客户服务成本，有能力在每周7天每天24小时的基础上处理客户需求以及与客户和合作伙伴建立更紧密的关系。

阶段2和阶段3：面向员工的战略。 就面向员工的过程而言，阶段2包括建立一个公司内部网，同时阶段3需要为专门的机构（如销售、客户服务、采购和财务等方面）开发和配置更强的网络工具。

中小企业在拥有公司内部网后能够通过内部的网络门户向员工传递利益、产品和商务信息，减少印刷文件并能够确保以更低的成本及时、一致地发布公司信息。内部网也为与远程和移动员工的沟通提供了一个更经济有效的方法。

开发和部署内部事务应用促进了更广泛的跨公司合作，同时也降低了新应用的设计、部署和培训费用，并且使得企业能够更加快速和有效地将新产品推向市场。员工们会觉得自己更有控制权，因为他们拥有更好的工具和更多的信息来处理客户需求。

阶段4：全面的电子商务实施。 阶段4即最后阶段，通过能够提供一站式购物、财务和设计服务等一系列服务，实现中小企业和合作伙伴网站的互通互联，使得面向顾客和员工的流程环路闭合。中小企业得益于利用合作伙伴的网站作为传递其产品和服务的新渠道，而客户则从可用的额外增值服务中获利。此外，借助合作伙伴的网站可以使中小企业将投资集中在其核心业务上。

匹配电子商务和你的目标

有效地销售、采购和获取资源是中小企业日常经营活动的关键流程，也是企业取得长期成功的根基所在。电子商务可以作为必不可少的强有力的发动机来推进这些持续进行的努力。但是，与所有核心业务的改进一样，这样的整合不可能立刻实现，这个过程需要有序地、逐步地变化，直至完成。

对大多数中小企业而言，开展有限的、定义清晰的电子商务计划，并与特定的商业动机和最高利益机会结合起来，将会更加成功，而且将产生更快、更切实的结果。一般情况下，开展电子商务不需要进行全面重组，重组需要一段时间才能得到最起码的回报。

Unit 8　How SMBs Can Profit from the Internet

　　与大多数商业投资一样，中小企业的技术投资最基本的目标是：满足基本的财务目标。无论是什么规模或行业的中小企业，为了成功所必须克服的最重要的问题都是非常一致的。

　　国际数据公司（IDC）询问过许多企业，什么是他们认为最重要的问题或关注点——实际上就是他们最担心的事情或者是那些让他们夜不能寐的问题。客户和员工所关注的问题经常被各种类型和规模的企业所提及。

　　毫不奇怪，获取新的客户并且为现有的客户更有效地工作，与诸如吸引并留住称职员工等内部问题同等重要。

　　电子商务通过在核心业务流程中利用简单却强有力的技术和工具，可以在其内部与外部实现高效运行。就外部而言，电子商务解决方案帮助中小企业更容易和更有效地满足和超越客户的需求；就内部而言，它能够帮助建立员工满意度、提高雇员的技能和生产率。

　　意义深远的是，中小企业感兴趣的是技术带来的价值，而不是技术本身。这就是为什么电子商务在帮助中小企业提升客户接触面和客户服务以及提高员工效率和满意度等方面这么有潜力的原因。

UNIT 9 Could My Business Be an E-Business

TEXT

Definition

A. There is a sharp line between companies that are capable of using Internet technologies and the web to spur innovation and those that are not. Do you have the desire, motivation and resources available to make e-business a reality?

Overview

B. Becoming an e-business requires considerable research, analysis and planning. Starting the process now could reap enormous benefits for you in the future. This unit will help you realize the steps that need to be taken in becoming an e-business:

(1) Identify the e-business opportunity;

(2) Plan your e-business;

(3) Build a business case for change;

(4) Manage the change.

Identify the E-Business Opportunity

C. When considering e-business, examine your customer and supplier relationships to see where you could add the greatest value to your business:

(1) What parts of your customer model are the weakest?

(2) Where could the greatest cost savings be made (for yourself and your customers)?

(3) How can you offer a better service than your competitors?

D. The more opportunities you can identify across your customer and supplier business models, the greater the justification for introducing e-business activities. Split your business operations into individual functions, and examine their e-business potential.

(1) Customer: market research; promotions; sales; operations; and after sales service.

(2) Sourcing: tenders; managing contracts; logistics; and payment & monitoring.

Plan Your E-Business

E. Know where your company is going and have a clear understanding of what is possible, what your business framework is and what your customers require.

F. Your company must define its e-business vision, state its objectives to achieve that vision, and plan the activities it will undertake to meet the stated objectives.

G. Identify the key objectives you will work towards. You need to consider what can be done quickly and what will bring the biggest net benefit:

(1) What are your priorities?

(2) Where are you currently losing money?

(3) What is the weakest link in your business?

(4) Are there any "quick wins"?

H. Deliver proof of benefits quickly, choosing the lowest risk and easiest option to implement.

I. Take incremental steps. E-business is about changing how you do business inside and outside the company. This involves change with customers, suppliers and business partners. It will mean opening up your systems to your staff, as well as to customers and suppliers.

Build a Business Case for Change

J. Consider the business case for proceeding.

K. Your justification for adopting e-business will be measured by the tangible and intangible benefits:

(1) Tangible: Increasing revenues; increasing margins; reducing purchasing costs; reducing transaction costs.

(2) Intangible: Enhancing customer service; improving business relationships; improving decision-making.

L. Tangible benefits, like the cost-saving benefits of e-business, are often the only justification that companies will address in deciding to implement new technologies or business services.

M. Do not, however, ignore some of the softer, more intangible benefits of adopting e-business. Providing direct customer order entry may save you money in transaction costs, but also offers a real benefit to customers who prefer the flexibility.

Manage the Change

N. Becoming an e-business is about management and leadership not technology. Managing technology is easy; changing people's attitudes and actions is harder.

O. Providing the right cultural environment for e-business to flourish is critical and a challenge for most companies. Assess your e-business environment based on the following questions:

(1) Is time made available for company-wide improvements?

(2) Are people informed of issues or changes?

(3) Are the appropriate stakeholders consulted in decision-making?

(4) Is there a clear understanding of customer requirements?

(5) Is there an organizational perspective on individual actions?

P. Your company's ability to change, adapt and respond to dynamic market conditions will depend on the desire, motivation and innovation of your staff.

Q. Be realistic. It may take longer than you anticipate to adopt e-business practices and fully exploit the opportunities that exist.

R. At the end of the day, what will make the difference in transforming your company will be the strength of your e-business vision and everyone's commitment to its principles.

Case Study

S. Nexfor was part of an initial programme of work, sponsored by Scottish Enterprise, to look at e-business within the Forestry Industry.

T. Nexfor first developed a vision "to implement and use technology to achieve profitable and sustainable growth…" and from this came their strategy and action plan for e-business. This was shared with their key suppliers and customers.

U. Initial efforts concentrated on developing web-based solutions for their customers to place and track orders; performance was closely related to ROI (Return On Investment) and customer service improvements.

V. E-business is now key for Nexfor, and from the early wins in terms of reducing paper costs, it had planned further initiatives, including XML-based (Extensible Mark-up Language based) supplier invoicing.

W. Nexfor is now at the forefront of e-business adoption within the Forestry Industry in Scotland.

Actions and Next Steps

X. Actions and next steps are as follows.

(1) Identify the e-business opportunity. E-business will succeed where: you differentiate your business proposition; you make it difficult for your competitors to imitate; your business is capable of exploiting the opportunities; and you make your business transparent to partners.

(2) Plan your e-business. Assess where your priorities are, where you are losing money, where quick wins are to be made. Focus on one functional area, e.g. procurement or after sales service, before tackling the rest of the organization.

(3) Build a business case for change. Assess the tangible and intangible benefits of your e-business projects. Measure your e-business initiatives against your reasons for implementation.

(4) Manage the change. Create an environment to motivate and innovate your e-business. Inform staff of changes, take time for company-wide improvements, understand your customers' needs and focus on the organization rather than the individual.

Words and Expressions

spur [spɜː(r)]	v.	激励，促进
reap [riːp]	v.	获得，收获（农作物）
justification [ˌdʒʌstɪfɪˈkeɪʃn]	n.	正当理由，合理的解释
tender [ˈtendə(r)]	v.	投标，参与竞标
logistics [ləˈdʒɪstɪks]	n.	后勤，物流
incremental [ˌɪnkrɪˈment(ə)l]	adj.	增加的，递增的
tackle [ˈtækl]	v.	应对，解决（难题或任务）
initiative [ɪˈnɪʃətɪv]	n.	倡议，主动性
invoicing [ˈɪnvɔɪsɪŋ]	n.	发货单，发票
availability [əˌveɪləˈbɪləti]	n.	可利用性，使用价值

Questions

Directions: In this section, you are required to answer the following questions according to the information in the text.

(1) What role can identifying the e-business opportunity play?

(2) How many steps a company need to plan its e-business?

(3) What are the tangible and intangible benefits?

(4) What is Nexfor's origin of planning further initiatives?

(5) What is Nexfor's situation within the Forestry Industry in Scotland at present?

Exercises

Directions: In this section, there are five questions and for each of them there are four choices marked A, B, C and D. You should decide on the best choice.

(1) Which of the following is not the requirements to become an e-business?

    A. Research   B. Analysis   C. Marketing   D. Planning

(2) Who will be involved with when changing the way a company does business inside and outside the e-business?

    A. Customers, staff and suppliers   B. Customers, suppliers and business partners

    C. Staff, suppliers and business partners   D. Staff, customers and business partners

(3) What is the only justification will companies often address in deciding to implement new technologies or business services?

    A. Customer service   B. Business relationships

    C. Decision-making   D. Cost-saving benefits of e-business

(4) Which of the following statements is true according to the passage?

    A. Becoming an e-business is about management and leadership just technology.

    B. Providing the right cultural environment is not important.

    C. Changing people's attitudes and actions is more difficult.

    D. Managing technology is a challenge for most companies.

(5) What is the vision Nexfor first developed?

    A. To implement and use technology to achieve profitable and sustainable growth.

    B. To make decisions about their strategy and action plan for e-business.

    C. To get the leading position within the Forestry Industry in Scotland.

    D. To evaluate their performance closely related to customer service improvements.

Unit 9　Could My Business Be an E-Business

Translation

我的业务能发展成电子商务吗

定　义

在那些可以利用互联网技术及网络来激发创新的企业和没有这一能力的企业之间存在着明显的界限。你是否有发展电子商务的期望、动力和可用资源呢？

概　述

实现电子商务需要大量的研究、分析及计划。现在开始实施，你将可以在未来收获丰厚。本单元将帮助你了解发展电子商务必须采取的几个步骤：
（1）识别发展电子商务的机遇；
（2）制订电子商务计划；
（3）创造适宜变化的商业情形；
（4）管理变化。

识别发展电子商务的机遇

在考虑发展电子商务时，应审视顾客、供应商的关系，找到可以为你的业务增加最多价值的地方：
（1）顾客模式中哪些方面最薄弱？
（2）哪些方面可以最大程度地降低成本（为公司及顾客）？
（3）怎样提供优于竞争对手的服务？
在顾客和供应商的商务模式中，识别的机会越多，就越适合发展电子商务。把整个业务流程按不同的职能划分开来，研究各自发展电子商务的潜能。
（1）从顾客角度划分：市场研究，促销，销售，运行，售后服务。
（2）从资源角度划分：投标，合同管理，物流，付款及监测。

制订你的电子商务计划

首先要了解公司的发展方向，清楚地知道哪些方面可以发展电子商务，公司的商业框架是什么以及顾客的需求是什么。

公司必须确立发展电子商务的长期愿景；继而确立实现长期愿景的短期目标；进而规划实现这些短期目标的行动。

确立要实现的主要短期目标。必须考虑哪些短期目标可以很快实现，哪些短期目标可以带来最大的净收益：

（1）公司的优势何在？
（2）公司哪些方面正处于亏本状态？
（3）业务环节中哪个环节最薄弱？
（4）有没有实现"快赢"的可能？

选择风险最小最简便的途径，快速找到盈利点。

逐步采取措施。电子商务意味着改变公司内外的商业运作模式，这一改变涉及公司与顾客、公司与供应商以及公司与商业伙伴关系的变化。电子商务同时意味着将公司的系统开放，不仅向公司员工开放，而且向顾客以及供应商开放。

创造适宜变化的商业情形

考虑一下未来的业务情形。

你对是否发展电子商务的判断取决于电子商务能带来多少有形或无形的收益。

（1）有形收益：增加收入，增加利润，减少采购成本，减少交易成本。
（2）无形收益：提高客户服务质量，改善商务关系，改进决策进程。

企业在决定使用新技术或提供新服务时，通常只会考虑电子商务可以节约成本等有形收益。

但在采用电子商务时，不能忽略一些相对更温和、更无形的利益。向顾客提供直接订购登录不但可以降低交易成本，而且可以为那些偏爱灵活性的顾客带来真正的便利。

管 理 变 化

建立电子商务重在管理和领导，而不是科技本身。运用技术容易，难的是改变人们的态度和行为。

为电子商务的快速发展提供一个恰当的文化环境至关重要，大多数公司都面临这样的挑战。根据以下问题评价公司发展电子商务的环境：

（1）若要改进整个公司的运作，时间安排上是否充裕？
（2）人们了解这些新情况和变化吗？
（3）在决策过程中是否与适当的利益相关者商议过？
（4）对顾客的需求是否有清晰的了解？
（5）对单个的活动是否有组织视角？

公司员工的愿望、动力及创新意识决定一个公司改变、适应并对动态的市场环境做出反应的能力。

要面对现实。实现电子商务模式并充分挖掘存在的机遇的时间可能会比预期的长。

最后，公司变革的成效取决于公司发展电子商务长期愿景的力量以及大家对这一原则的投入。

案 例 分 析

Nexfor是苏格兰企业赞助的初步工作计划的一部分，该计划旨在探索林业电子商务发展之路。

Nexfor首先建立起"实施和利用科技实现利润持续增长……"这样的愿景，并由此制订出发展电子商务的策略和行动计划。这是与他们的主要供应商和客户共享的。

初步工作重点是为顾客设计订购及追踪订单的基于网络的解决方案，工作绩效与投资回报（ROI）及顾客服务质量的改善密切相关。

现在，电子商务对Nexfor来说已经非常重要。早期目标是降低纸张成本，之后又设定了进一步的目标，包括基于可扩展标志性语言（XML）的供应商货品发票。

Nexfor现在已经成了苏格兰林业领域采用电子商务的"领头羊"。

行动及进一步举措

（1）确定电子商务机会。电子商务将在以下几种情况下取得成功：你的业务主张与众不同，你的竞争对手难以模仿你，你的企业可以挖掘机遇，你的业务对合作伙伴透明。

（2）制订电子商务计划。评估企业的优势所在，估计哪些方面会亏本，哪些领域可以实现"快赢"。先聚焦某个职能领域，比如采购部或售后服务，然后再处理组织中的其余部分。

（3）创造适宜变化的情形。评估电子商务项目的有形收益、无形收益。根据发展电子商务的理由衡量电子商务计划。

（4）管理变化。创造一个适合的环境，促进电子商务的发展与创新。让员工了解到这种变化，花时间改善整个公司的运作，了解顾客的需求，着眼于整个组织体系而不是单一的个体。

Chapter 4 E-Business about Industries
第4篇 行业电子商务

- UNIT 10　Retail E-Procurement: Minimizing Costs and Improving Productivity

- UNIT 11　Selling Products on Facebook: The Emergence of Social Commerce

- UNIT 12　What Do Consumers Really Want?

UNIT 10 Retail E-Procurement: Minimizing Costs and Improving Productivity

Introduction

A. The inflation and subsequent deflation of the dot-com era and a tougher economic climate are forcing retailers to focus on "back to basics" execution of their business strategies. While many companies are wary, industry leaders are looking to build e-business capabilities that drive real and lasting value.

B. While e-commerce euphoria was largely driven by the fear of lost market share, the e-business strategies of today are seeking sustainable competitive advantage. Electronic procurement (e-procurement) can be a primary source of competitive advantage for retailers in:

(1) Reducing or avoiding costs and improving productivity by eliminating manual, paper-based processes and empowering employee procurement within a controlled set of parameters.

(2) Enforcing on-contract buying by providing an easy-to-use tool that automatically puts procurement standards and business rules into effect.

(3) Developing reporting capabilities that provide a consolidated record of spending, supplier performance and transaction costs, which can then be used for strategic sourcing, contract negotiation and supplier relationship management.

(4) Reducing purchasing cycle times and effort by streamlining procurement processes.

Enter E-Procurement

C. E-procurement is a prudent advancement in the quest to create a highly efficient virtual value chain, where complex transactions become a fluid, collaborative process between buyers and sellers. E-procurement continues the trend toward process automation and replacement of manual labor through information technology. By automating processes, like requisitioning approval and payment, e-procurement essentially eliminates the need for human intervention.

E-Procurement Models

D. The expensive and frequently complex world of one-to-one EDI exchanges and supplier enablement is unlikely to survive long in the "cheaper, faster" online world. While electronic procurement can at first seem complex and confusing, lower-cost benefits and continuous availability will ultimately win the day. Already, e-procurement has developed into several major public and private models for buyers and suppliers looking for better ways to handle their basic procurement processes.

E. Private Models

(1) Supply-side—A company creates its own online catalog that allows a number of buyers to browse and purchase products online with real-time, contract-specific buying tools.

(2) Buy-side—In this model, the buyer maintains the online catalogs and databases of multiple suppliers' goods and services, and is responsible for tying all transactions into those companies' purchasing and financial systems.

F. Public Models

(1) Independent trading exchanges—In this model, an independent website provides the entry point for multiple buyers and sellers to transact business for a fee or on a subscription basis.

(2) Vertical trading exchanges—This model typically focuses on the needs of one industry, with sponsorship provided by one or more industry leaders.

(3) Horizontal trading exchanges—This model cuts across industry boundaries and focuses on broad categories of goods and services that are common to many companies.

(4) Auctions—Electronic auctions, which are a subset of online trading exchanges, provide online, real-time exchange of goods through a forum in which buyers or sellers log on and make offers against a request. They can be private or public in form.

Unit 10　Retail E-Procurement: Minimizing Costs and Improving Productivity

Third-Party Procurement Service Models

G. Third-party procurement services typically offer a hosted, buy-side solution—a private procurement model for enhancing supply chain efficiency and maximizing savings without incurring significant costs.

H. In the third-party procurement service model, the service provider builds and manages the online catalogs, often providing leveraged pricing by aggregating its subscribers' buying power.

Expected Results

I. What can you expect from "e-procurement"?

J. Online procurement can completely transform the way retailers purchase goods, making process efficiencies and permanently lower costs not only possible, but affordable to achieve.

K. Today, most company purchasing of indirect materials is done by telephone (85%), fax (65%) and face-to-face discussions with suppliers (50%).

L. To understand the scale of what automating purchasing process can do, consider data offered by those who have initiated strong "e-procurement" programs:

(1) Average transaction costs dropped from USD 107 to USD 30.8.

(2) Cycle times dipped from 7.3 days to 2 days.

(3) Average costs of generating an order fell from USD 35 to less than a single dollar.

(4) Direct purchasing costs dropped from USD 60 to USD 5.11.

(5) The number of full-time purchasing employees plummeted from 29 to 2.

Clearly, "e-procurement" can have a dramatic effect on a retailer's bottom line.

Words and Expressions

procurement [prəˈkjʊrmənt]	n.	获得（军需品等的）行为
execution [ˌeksɪˈkjuːʃn]	n.	执行，处死
euphoria [juːˈfɔːriə]	n.	狂喜
parameter [pəˈræmɪtər]	n.	参数，界定
empower [ɪmˈpaʊər]	v.	授权，使能够
consolidated [kənˈsɑːlɪdeɪtɪd]	adj.	巩固的；合并的
cycle time		周转时间

aggregate ['ægrɪgeɪt]	v.	聚集，集合，合计
permanently ['pɜːrmənəntlɪ]	adv.	永存地，不变地
plummet ['plʌmɪt]	v.	垂直落下

Questions

***Directions:** In this section, you are required to answer the following questions according to the information in the text.*

(1) According to the author, why should we focus on e-procurement in retail?

(2) Why is e-procurement a prudent advancement in terms of creating a highly efficient virtual value chain?

(3) How does e-procurement eliminate the need for human intervention?

(4) What are the e-procurement models introduced in this unit?

(5) What can we expect from e-procurement?

Exercises

***Directions:** In this section, you are going to read ten statements attached to the text. Each statement contains information given in one of the paragraphs in the text. Identify the paragraph from which the information is derived. You may choose a paragraph more than once.*

(1) Online procurement can fully change the way retailers purchase goods.

(2) While many companies are worried, leading industries are looking to build e-bussiness capabilities.

(3) At present, most transactions of purchasing are done by telephone.

(4) "E-procurement" can reduce purchasing cycle times and effort by streamlining procurement processes.

(5) "E-procurement" progresses toward process automation and replacement of human labor through information technology.

(6) An independent website provides the entry point for many buyers and sellers to transact business.

(7) E-procurement can be an effective and competitive source for retailers.

(8) Providing leveraged pricing by aggregating its subscribers' buying power, the third-party procurement service provider builds and manages the online catalogs.

(9) The costly and frequently complex world of one-to-one EDI exchanges and supplier enablement cannot survive long in the online world.

(10) E-procurement can have a heavy impact on a retailer's bottom line.

Translation

零售业电子采购分析：成本最小化，提高生产力

前言

网络热潮时代的泡沫经济以及随之而来的经济萧条，加上日益严峻的经济形势，迫使零售商不得不把目光又集中在"回归基本"的商务执行战略上。当很多公司非常谨慎小心不敢越雷池半步的时候，产业"领头羊"正努力构建电子商务体系，这一体系能够带来真实的和持久的利润。

虽然电子商务过热的最大驱动力源于企业对失去市场份额的担心，但今天的电子商务战略正在寻找可持续的竞争优势。对零售业来说，电子采购可以在以下方面成为其竞争优势的主要来源：

（1）通过减少手工的、基于纸面的流程，并授权员工通过一整套参数进行采购，可以达到降低成本、避免浪费、提高生产力的目的。

（2）通过提供简单易用的工具，实现采购标准与商业规则的自动化处理，以增强按合同购买的能力。

（3）建立报告功能，该功能可提供一个关于支出、供应商表现和交易成本的综合记录，这个记录可以用于战略采购、合同谈判以及供应商关系的管理等。

（4）通过精简采购流程，可以减少采购周期和工作量。

开始电子采购

电子采购是寻求建立高效的虚拟价值链的一个审慎的进步，它使得复杂的交易变成买卖者之间一个流畅的协作过程。电子采购继续朝向程序自动化和通过信息技术代替手工劳动这样一个趋势迈进。通过自动化程序，如申请审批和支付，电子采购从根本上消除了人为的干预。

电子采购模型

在"更便宜、更快捷"的网络世界中,成本高昂且程序复杂的一对一的EDI交易和供应商协同软件是很难长期生存下去的。尽管电子采购乍看起来似乎复杂且令人困惑,但其凭借更低成本的收益和持续的有效性最终将赢得未来。目前,电子采购领域中已经为那些寻求更好方法来处理基本采购流程的采购商和供应商开发出了一些主要的公共模型和私用模型。

私用模型

(1)卖方平台——一个公司创建它自己的在线目录,允许一系列买家在线浏览并通过实时的合同专用购买工具在线购买他们的产品。

(2)买方平台——在这个模型中,买方维护各供货商货物和服务信息的在线目录和数据库,并负责把所有的交易与公司的采购与财务系统联系起来。

公共模型

(1)独立贸易交易平台——在这一模型中,由一个独立的网站为多个买主和卖主开展交易业务提供入口,平台为此收取费用或提供订阅服务。

(2)垂直贸易平台——这一模型主要关注一个行业的需要,并且由一个或多个行业领导者发起。

(3)水平贸易平台——这一模型打破了行业间的界限,并集中于很多公司都需要的多种类的货物和服务。

(4)拍卖——电子拍卖,是在线贸易交易的一个子集,通过论坛的形式提供在线、实时的商品交易,在这一论坛中,采购商或销售商注册登录,并且针对需求请求出价。其在形式上可分为公共或私用两种模式。

第三方采购服务模型

第三方采购服务,通常提供一个托管的买方解决方案——这是一个私用的采购模型,它在不增加高额成本的前提下提高供应链效率,并且最大化节约成本。

在第三方采购服务模型中,服务提供商创建和管理在线目录,经常通过聚集客户购买力来提供杠杆定价。

期望的结果

你期望从电子采购中获得什么?

Unit 10   Retail E-Procurement: Minimizing Costs and Improving Productivity

在线采购能够完全颠覆零售商采购商品的方式，使流程高效化，并永久性地降低成本，这不但在理论上成为可能而且实践起来成本不会太高。

现在，大多数公司是通过电话（85%）、传真（65%）和面对面与供应商讨论（50%）的方式购买间接材料。

为了理解采购流程自动化可以在多广的范围内起作用，我们可以参考以下数据，这些数据由已经发起强大电子采购计划的厂商提供：

（1）平均交易成本从107美元降低至30.8美元；

（2）周期时间从7.3天降到2天；

（3）生成一份订单的平均成本从35美元降低至不超过1美元；

（4）直接采购成本从60美元降低至5.11美元；

（5）专职采购的雇员数量从29人骤减至2人。

显然，电子采购对零售商的盈亏平衡点产生了巨大影响。

UNIT 11

Selling Products on Facebook: The Emergence of Social Commerce

TEXT

The Importance of Facebook Commerce for E-Commerce Businesses

A. It is no secret that Facebook dominates the social networking field (see Table 11.1). Facebook controls more than half of the US traffic to social media sites and has more than 500 million active users who together spend over 700 billion minutes per month on the site. Facebook is now taking on e-commerce, and changing the way that people shop online and interact on social media sites.

Table 11.1   Top 5 Social Networking Sites

(US market share of visits on September 2010)

Facebook	YouTube	MySpace	Twitter	LinkedIn
61.47%	16.61%	6.44%	1.87%	1.25%

B. Facebook commerce (F-commerce), the ability for merchants to sell products directly from their Facebook fan page via the creation of a "shop" tab, is one of the fastest growing subsets of social commerce. The Facebook shopping experience gives users the ability to view a product catalog, read reviews, make a purchase, and interact with their friends, all from a company's Facebook fan page.

C. An October 2010 Vertical Rail study found that 87 of Internet Retailer's top 100 retailers had a Facebook fan page with a combined 36 million fans. However, of these 100 companies, only four offer a "shop" tab on their Facebook. This illustrates that merchants have done the legwork to develop their social networks and build their fanbase, but only a few have taken social commerce to the next step, using F-commerce to turn fans into customers.

The Benefits of Selling Products on Facebook for E-Commerce Businesses

D. Facebook commerce gives merchants the opportunity to succeed by using this viral selling platform to maximize the results of their social media efforts. The followings are just some of the ways that selling products on Facebook can benefit E-commerce merchants.

Increase online sales

E. According to a report by eMarketer, frequent Facebook users spend an average of USD 67 online, compared to the average of USD 50 spent by occasional Facebook visitors and USD 27 spent by non-Facebook users. This means that by allowing consumers to shop directly from Facebook, merchants are targeting a highly profitable segment of active online shoppers.

Demonstrable ROI

F. According to an August 2009 survey by Mzinga and Babson Executive Education, 84% of business social media programs don't measure return on investment. Many of the Facebook shopping applications provide detailed analytics to give merchants deeper insight into the strengths, weakness, and overall health of their social media marketing program.

Build brand awareness

G. Many of the businesses currently selling products on Facebook require users to "like" the brand before they can begin shopping (see Fig. 11.1 and Fig. 11.2). Once someone "likes" the business, their entire network is notified, prompting more Facebook users to check out the site and repeat the process. The result is that Facebook users are constantly seeing your company and products in their News Feed, increasing brand awareness and recognition.

Fig. 11.1 Nine West "Like"

Fig. 11.2   Levi's "Like"

The Benefits of Selling Products on Facebook for Consumers

H. Facebook commerce provides a unique experience for online shoppers, giving fans access to Facebook-only sales, exclusive coupons, and sneak peeks at unreleased products. Here are just a few ways that consumers can benefit from shopping on Facebook.

Convenience

I. By combining shopping and social media, consumers no longer have to jump from site to site trying to research a product, make a purchase, and connect with their friends. When consumers shop on Facebook, they are able to ask the opinions of their friends and can share purchases or wish lists with the rest of their social network. Facebook commerce allows shoppers to research, shop, and share without leaving the Facebook site.

Fig. 11.3   Specials for Facebook Fans

Special discounts and coupons

J. According to a June 2010 study from Compete, more than half of consumers who used a coupon during their last online purchase would not have bought the item without it. The study also found that consumers who use coupons or purchase items on sale actually spend more money and are more satisfied with the shopping experience. By providing coupons and specials for Facebook fans (see Fig. 11.3), merchants are providing something interesting, exclusive, and valuable to their customers.

Unit 11 Selling Products on Facebook: The Emergence of Social Commerce

Read reviews and comments

K. An August 2010 survey from ChannelAdvisor found that 83% of shoppers are influenced by customer reviews. Online shoppers rely heavily on ratings and reviews to guide their purchasing decisions, so it is essential that merchants have this information readily accessible. Shoppers using Facebook are able to read product ratings and reviews directly from the company's fan page (see Fig. 11.4), without having to visit a third-party rating and review site.

Fig. 11.4　Facebook Reviews and Comments

Facebook Commerce Applications

L. In order for merchants to sell products on Facebook, they must first install an application that creates a "shop" tab on their fan page. Currently, only a handful of companies provide F-commerce applications. Some companies offer flat-fee services, while others operate on a revenue-share pricing model. A few of the applications allow consumers to complete the entire checkout process on Facebook, while others transfer the shopper back to the company website to finish the transaction.

M. The following five companies are leaders in this new industry. Each offers a unique Facebook application that benefits both businesses and consumers. These companies offer a variety of pricing and structural options, ensuring that there is a solution for every size and type of company.

Milyoni (Million-eye)

N. Milyoni helps integrate E-commerce business with social media in a "conversational commerce" site that operates on a performance driven pricing model. Milyoni offers a managed solution instead of a software download, and they provide the necessary technology, hosting, and customer service to ensure a successful Facebook store integration (see Fig. 11.5). The goal of Milyoni is not only to increase online sales through a Facebook store, but also to connect fans in a social context to promote customer engagement and loyalty.

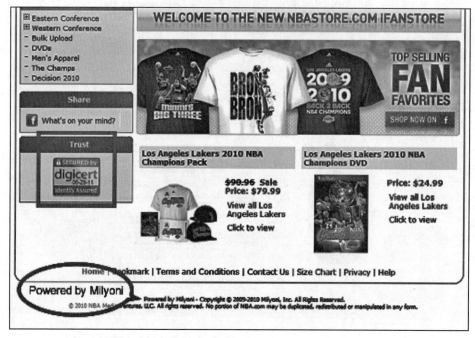

Fig. 11.5　Milyoni Integration for Facebook Store

O. Dean Alms, VP of Strategy and Marketing at Milyoni believes that what makes Milyoni unique is their "very innovative set of social merchandising tools including the ability to do image posts, audio posts, and video posts. Each of these posts allows you to engage with your customers first in topics of interest and follow up with a commerce opportunity". Milyoni has recently added a new feature to their social merchandising arsenal, called Instant Showcase (see Fig. 11.6), which allows a fan to purchase a product directly from their News Feed with as few as three or four clicks.

Payvment

P. Currently in its beta stage, Payvment offers a free shopping application for merchants who want to sell products directly from Facebook. Merchants using Payvment will benefit from the easy installation process, integrated marketing features, and built-in sales tracking. Payvment allows merchants to sell an unlimited number of products and offers domestic and international

Unit 11 Selling Products on Facebook: The Emergence of Social Commerce

shipping options. Their promotional features include Facebook fan discounts, the ability to "share" store and item information with Facebook friends, and built in review and commenting capabilities (see Fig 11.7).

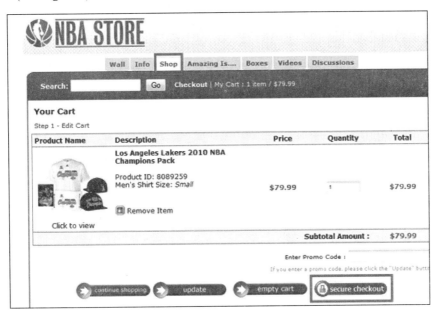

Fig. 11.6 Instant Showcase

Fig. 11.7 Payvment Features

Q. According to Christian Taylor, CEO of Payvment, the most important feature they offer merchants and consumers is their Facebook-wide shopping network. He explained, "When you launch a store on Facebook using Payvment, your products are available to be discovered across the entire network of Facebook stores." Over 30,000 stores with over 200 new store launching daily. Plus, if a Facebook user leaves your Facebook store without purchasing the items in their cart, they can complete their purchase across the entire network. Only Payvment provides the Facebook-wide shopping solution (see Fig 11.8).

Fig. 11.8 Complete Purchace via Payvment

ShopFans

R. ShopFans is a social commerce application created by Adgregate Markets (see Fig. 11.9). Their pricing is based on revenue share and is unique to each client. The ShopFans application allows merchants to sell products directly on their Facebook Fan page, and consumers can complete the entire secure transaction without leaving the Facebook site (see Fig. 11.10). This application allows businesses to market to their social networks and gives shoppers the ability to post products on their wall, sign up for registries, and participate in exclusive sales. Their goal is to turn "conversations into conversions" by fully integrating social commerce with E-commerce to create a unique shopping experience.

Unit 11 Selling Products on Facebook: The Emergence of Social Commerce

Fig. 11.9 ShopFans Application

Fig. 11.10 ShopFans Transaction

S. When it comes to shopping on Facebook, one of the primary concerns for consumers is privacy and security. Henry Wong, CEO of Adgregate Markets explained that, "Adgregate Markets's ShopFans is the only social commerce solution secured by McAfee, the exclusive provider of consumer security software to Facebook, and TRUSTe. This solution enables e-retailers to have a custom Facebook store, secured by McAfee and TRUSTe that utilizes all of Facebook's social plumbing."

ShopTab

T. Merchants using ShopTab (see Fig. 11.11) can choose from three different pricing options (USD 10/500 products, USD 15/1,000 products, or USD 20/5,000 products) with no long term contract, no set up fee or any percentage of revenue when setting up their Facebook application—only a month to month membership fee. When shoppers are ready to check out from the merchant's ShopTab page, they are taken to the actual business website instead of paying directly through Facebook (see Fig. 11.12). This transition from Facebook to merchant website removes any worry of payment delay or security breach and has proven to be an amazing website traffic generator from the over 500 million Facebook fans. With a low monthly cost and easy self-management tools, ShopTab is a great way to get involved in Facebook commerce with almost no risk. ShopTab also integrates Facebook social sharing for each product to help merchants gain awareness among other Facebook users.

Fig. 11.11 ShopTab Page

Unit 11 Selling Products on Facebook: The Emergence of Social Commerce

Fig. 11.12   Website Transition

U. ShopTab prides itself of being simple for both merchants and customers. ShopTab's Co-Founder, Jay Feitlinger cited the low cost, customer focus, data feed upload based off Google Base platform, and automatic scheduled updates for merchants who require daily pricing and inventory changes completed automatically as the benefits that set ShopTab apart. He explained, "We took the time to understand how customers want to engage with a shopping tab on Facebook and made sure that the usability provided the best experience possible. ShopTab was also the first Facebook commerce application that allowed merchants to upload a data feed that immediately published product information such as price and description, as well as pulled in product images so merchants don't have to take the time to upload each individual product image." In addition, with ShopTab retailers don't have to worry that other competitors' products will show on their ShopTab because only their products will show on their Facebook ShopTab.

SocialShop

V. SocialShop operates on the belief that combining social media and E-commerce leads to more customers and more sales. SocialShop, created by Big Commerce, offers five programs that range from USD 24.95/month to USD 299.95/ month with a USD 49.95 startup fee. SocialShop is easy to use and connects merchants and customers in a social context by allowing Facebook users to browse products through a "Shop" tap on the business fan page, view product photos, and quickly share products with friends (see Fig. 11.13).

W. Mitchell Harper, Co-Founder and Co-CEO of Big Commerce believes that the ease of use makes SocialShop stand out from other F-commerce applications (see Fig. 11.14). He

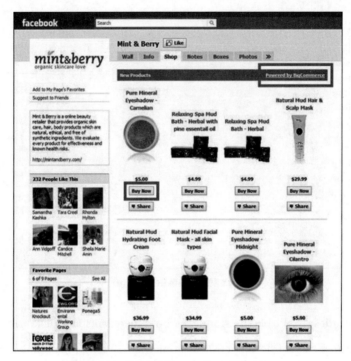

Fig. 11.13 "Shop" Tap on SocialShop Page

Fig. 11.14 SocialShop Page

Unit 11 Selling Products on Facebook: The Emergence of Social Commerce

explained, "Merchants can add the application to Facebook and have it completely configured to show their products in less than two minutes. Their fans can not only browse products directly on Facebook, but they can also share the products on their wall. This is an excellent, form of viral marketing."

Facebook Commerce Strategy for E-commerce Businesses

X. The secret to a successful Facebook commerce strategy is to come up with interesting ways to involve your audience and add value to their shopping experience. Like most marketing and sales channels, one size does not fit all, so each company needs a unique F-commerce strategy to maximize the success of their "shop" tab. The following five strategies can help you effectively engage your fans and involve with F-commerce the right way.

Identify your fan base demographics

Y. Each F-commerce strategy should be customized so that it appeals to the interests and preferences of your specific Facebook fan base. Erica Terrell, Sr. Marketing Manager at Adgregate Markets believes that the key for merchants selling products on Facebook is to, "Identify their fan base demographics and try to engage them according to their interests." By understanding exactly who you are communicating with, you will be able to truly connect with your fans and create a successful F-commerce marketing campaign.

Focus on the news feed

Z. People are on Facebook to socialize, see what their friends are doing, look at pictures—they are not on Facebook to shop. Dean Alms, VP of Strategy and Marketing at Milyoni explained that, "The vast majority of time is spent on the News Feed. Facebook users are not going to find your store and ultimately buy products from you unless you engage them in the News Feed." Engaging your fans on their News Feed can include anything that adds to the conversation, whether that is posting interesting status updates, uploading new pictures, or commenting on other people's pages.

Turn fans into evangelists

I. Selling products on Facebook provides merchants with an interesting sales channel that combines marketing, sales, and interaction. According to Jay Feitlinger, CEO of ShopTab, when a company actively engages customers through a Facebook store, "The fans become evangelists, using Facebook to help in spreading the word about the products you sell. When you can start the shopping process right where people talk about it, the time and energy to get a consumer from awareness to an actual purchase is shortened."

Incentivize

II. According to Christian Taylor, CEO of Payvment, "Exclusive deals and sales from your Facebook page can be huge for driving interest and building fans." Merchants can incentivize product sales on Facebook by providing access to new product launches, Facebook specific coupons and specials, or distressed inventory sales. These exclusive events add to the viral component of Facebook commerce that is unparalleled by any other form of advertising.

Be transparent

III. Retailers have worked hard to develop their Facebook base and gain the trust of their fans. Now that social media is becoming commercial, it is essential that merchants maintain that trust by respecting their Fans. Mitchell Harper, Co-Founder and Co-CEO of Big Commerce reminds merchants, "The key is transparency. Don't look at Facebook as another way to 'sell' your customers. Instead, look at Facebook as a way to build transparent relationships with both customers and prospects."

The Future of F-commerce

IV. No matter how successful Facebook commerce becomes, it is essential to remember that Facebook is a social networking site, not a shopping site. Dean Alms compared Facebook commerce to going to a baseball game, "You are there to enjoy a ballgame, but during the game you are likely to buy some food, beverage and maybe even a ball cap or T-shirt. You never went there to 'shop'. Those that appreciate this role of Facebook will do better in the future than those that see Facebook as just another e-commerce channel."

V. In this early stage, it is unclear how this new sales channel will evolve and grow in the future. Both Jay Feitlinger and Mitchell Harper believe that Facebook Credits (Facebook's virtual currency) will play a significant role in future of F-commerce, while Erica Terrell predicts big changes in brand marketing strategies. All agree that Facebook commerce is about to revolutionize the way we shop, making it a truly social experience. The question is—how will your business take advantage of this exciting new opportunity?

Unit 11 Selling Products on Facebook: The Emergence of Social Commerce

Words and Expressions

legwork ['legwɜːk]	n.	〈口〉跑腿的活儿；吃力不讨好的活儿
coupon ['kuːpɔn]	n.	优惠券，（报纸、杂志附的）传单
sneak peeks		先睹为快，偷窥
merchandising ['mɜːtʃəndaɪzɪŋ]	n.	销售规划，附带商品
arsenal ['ɑːsənəl]	n.	武器，军火库
inventory ['ɪnvəntri]	n.	存货；清单
configure [kən'fɪgə]	vt.	配置
demography [dɪ'mɒgrəfi]	n.	人口学；人口统计学
evangelist [ɪ'vændʒəlɪst]	n.	（基督教）布道者；福音作者
incentivize [ɪn'sentɪvaɪz]	v.	鼓励

Questions

Directions: In this section, you are required to answer the following questions according to the information in the text.

(1) Why does F-commerce play a dominant role in the social networking field?

(2) What is Instant Showcase?

(3) Which company is the only one that provides the Facebook-wide shopping solution?

(4) Do consumers pay directly through Facebook when shoppers are ready to check out?

(5) According to Mitchell Harper, what makes SocialShop stand out from other F-commerce applications?

Exercises

Directions: In this section, you are required to answer the questions with T or F.
T (for True) if the statement agrees with the information given in the passage;
F (for False) if the statement contradicts the information given in the passage.

(1) Facebook controls more than half of the US traffic to social media sites and has more than 700 million active users who together spend over 500 billion minutes per month on the site.

(2) According to a study, merchants have done the legwork to develop their social networks and build their fan base, but only a few have used F-commerce to turn fans into customers.

(3) F-commerce gives merchants the opportunity to succeed by using the viral selling platform to minimize the results of their social media efforts.

(4) Few businesses presently selling products on Facebook require users to "like" the brand before they can begin shopping.

(5) Many consumers who used a coupon during their last online purchase would not have bought the item without it.

(6) Online shoppers rely slightly on ratings and reviews to guide their purchasing decisions, so it is not important that merchants have this information readily accessible.

(7) Merchants using Payvment will benefit from the easy installation process, integrated marketing features, and built-in sales tracking.

(8) The pricing in Milyoni is based on revenue share and is unique to each client.

(9) Facebook users are going to find your store and ultimately buy products form you unless you engage them in the News Feed.

(10) No matter how successful Facebook commerce becomes, it is essential to remember that Facebook is a shopping site, not a social networking site.

Unit 11 Selling Products on Facebook: The Emergence of Social Commerce

Translation

在脸书上销售产品：社交商务的出现

脸书商务对电子商务业务的重要性

毋庸置疑，脸书在社交网络领域占据主导地位（见表11.1）。脸书控制了美国一半以上的社交媒体网站流量，拥有5亿多活跃用户，这些用户平均每月在网站上活动的时间超过7,000亿分钟。目前脸书正在进军电子商务领域，并改变着人们网上购物以及在社交媒体网站上互动的方式。

表11.1 五大顶尖社交网站
2010年9月美国访问量的市场份额

脸书	油管	聚友	推特	领英
61.47%	16.61%	6.44%	1.87%	1.25%

脸书商务（F-commerce），即商家通过在脸书粉丝网页上创建一个"商店"选项卡来直接销售他们的产品，这是社交商务中增长最快的子集之一。脸书的购物给用户提供了查看产品目录、阅读评价、购物以及与朋友互动的功能，这些功能都来自公司的脸书粉丝网页。

在一项2010年10月份的垂直铁路（Vertical Rail）研究发现，网络零售商的前100强企业中有87家都各自拥有脸书粉丝网页，共拥有3,600万名粉丝。然而，在这100家公司中，仅仅有4家在他们的脸书上提供"商店"这个选项卡。这表明了商家已经为开发社交网络并建立粉丝基础铺好了路，但只有少数公司进行了社交商务的下一步：利用F-commerce将粉丝转变成顾客。

在脸书上销售产品对电子商务业务的益处

脸书商务让商家有机会利用病毒式的销售平台，最大化他们社交媒体的努力成果，给商家提供了成功的机会。以下是通过在脸书上销售产品使电子商务商家受益的几个方面。

增加网上销售

根据一份电子营销公司的研究报告，脸书的偶尔使用者平均消费50美元，非脸书用户平均消费27美元，而脸书的频繁使用者平均在线花费67美元。这意味着通过允许消费者直接在脸书上购物，商家正在把目标瞄向活跃的在线购物人群中非常有利可图的这部分对象。

显而易见的投资回报率

根据Mzinga和Babson高层经理培训项目2009年8月的一项调查，84%的商务社交媒体项目都不衡量投资回报率。很多脸书购物应用给商家提供了详细的分析方法，能够使商家更深入地了解社交媒体营销计划的优势、劣势以及总体健康状况。

建立品牌知名度

目前许多在脸书上销售产品的企业都要求用户在开始购物之前就要"赞"这个品牌（见图11.1和图11.2）。一旦有人"赞"某个企业，他们的整个关系网络就会被通知，这会促使更多的脸书用户访问该网站并重复这个过程。结果就是脸书上的用户不断地在消息推送中看到该企业及其产品信息，这就提升了品牌的知名度和品牌识别度。

图11.1 玖熙品牌"赞"网页

图11.2 李维斯品牌"赞"网页

在脸书上销售产品对消费者的益处

脸书商务为网上购物者提供了独特的体验，让粉丝们获得脸书的独家销售、独家优惠券以及提前浏览还未发布的产品的入口。以下是消费者在脸书上购物能够受益的几个方面。

Unit 11　Selling Products on Facebook: The Emergence of Social Commerce

便利性

通过将购物和社交媒体相结合，消费者再也不需要从一个网站跳到另一个网站去研究产品和购买，或者与他们的朋友联系。当消费者在脸书上购物时，他们能够询问自己朋友的意见，并可以与社交网络的其他成员分享购物体验或心愿清单。脸书商务允许购物者无须离开脸书网站就可以研究产品、购物以及分享体验。

特别折扣和优惠券

根据Compete 2010年6月的一项研究，超过一半的在上一次网上购物时使用了优惠券的消费者表示，如果没有优惠券则不会购买该产品。研究还发现，使用优惠券或购买打折的产品的消费者实际上花费了更多的钱，但购物体验更满意。通过为脸书的粉丝提供优惠券和特别商品（见图11.3），商家为客户提供了一些有趣的、专属的以及有价值的商品。

阅读评论和意见

ChannelAdvisor 2010年8月的调查发现，83%的购物者会受到顾客评论的影响。网上购物者很大程度上依赖商品打分和评论来指导他们的

图 11.3　脸书特别折扣

购买决策。因此，对商家来说，让这些信息很容易被访问是至关重要的。使用脸书的购物者可以直接从该公司的粉丝页面上阅读产品的等级和评论（见图11.4），而无须访问第三方等级和评论网站。

图 11.4　脸书评论

脸书商务应用

商家为了在脸书上推销他们的产品,必须先安装一个应用,以便在粉丝页面上添加一个"商店"标签。目前,只有少数公司提供脸书商务应用。一些公司提供固定收费服务,而其他公司则使用收入—份额定价模型。一部分应用允许消费者在脸书上完成整个结账过程,然而其他的应用则将顾客转移到公司网站完成交易。

以下五家公司是这个新产业中的"领头羊"。每家公司都提供了一个有利于企业和消费者的独特的脸书应用。这些公司提供各式各样的定价和结构选择,确保每种规模和类型的公司都有一个解决方案。

Milyoni(Million-eye)

Milyoni将电子商务企业与社交媒体整合在"对话式商业"网站上,该网站采用以绩效为驱动的定价模型进行运作。Milyoni提供了一个取代软件下载的可管理的解决方案,以及必要的技术、主机托管和客户服务以确保脸书商店的成功集成(见图11.5)。Milyoni的目标不仅是通过脸书商店增加网上销售,更是在社交环境中连接粉丝以提升顾客的参与度和忠诚度。

Milyon的战略和营销副总裁迪恩·阿尔姆斯认为,Milyoni的独特之处是"非常富有创新精神的社交推销工具集,具备对图像、音频和视频进行发布处理的能力。每一个这样的发布都能让你首先参与到你的顾客感兴趣的话题中,然后创造一个商业机遇"。Milyon最近在他们的社会化的商务集成中增加了一项新的功能,叫作"即时展示(Instant Showcase)"(见图11.6),这使得粉丝只需在消息推送中点击三四下鼠标就可以直接购买产品。

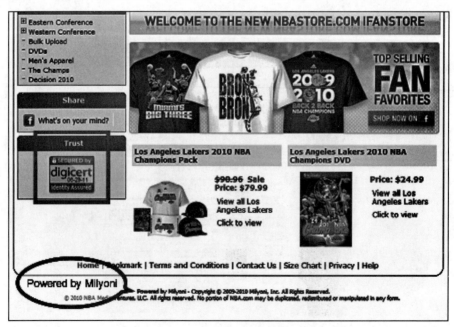

图 11.5　Milyoni 提供的脸书商店集成

Unit 11　Selling Products on Facebook: The Emergence of Social Commerce

图 11.6　即时展示

Payvment

目前Payvment在测试阶段,并向那些想直接在脸书上销售商品的商家们提供了一个免费的购物应用。使用Payvment的商家将受益于简易的安装过程、整合的营销功能与内置的销售跟踪。Payvment允许商家出售不限数量的商品,并提供国内和国际航运发货选项。他们的促销功能包括脸书粉丝折扣,跟脸书朋友"分享"商店和产品信息,以及内置的审查和评论(见图11.7)。

根据Payvment的首席执行官克里斯蒂安·泰勒的介绍,他们提供给商家和消费者最重要的功能就是他们的"泛脸书"的购物网络。他解释说:"当你使用Payvment在脸书上开一家商店时,你的产品在脸书商店的整个网络上都是可以被见到的。"Payvment已经拥有超过30,000家的商家,并且每天会有200家以上的新店注册。此外,如果一个脸书用户离开了你的脸书商店但并没有购买购物车里的商品,他们能通过整个网络完成购买。只有Payvment提供了"泛脸书"的购物解决方案(见图11.8)。

ShopFans

ShopFans是由Adgregate Markets创建的一种社交商务应用(见图11.9)。他们的定价基于收益份额,并且是每一位客户所独有的。ShopFans应用允许商家在脸书粉丝网页上直接销售他们的商品,并且消费者在不离开脸书网站的条件下可以安全地完成整个交易(见图11.10)。这个应用允许商家向他们的社交网络进行营销,并给予消费者在空间里发布商品、报名注册和独家销售的能力。他们的目标就是通过社交商务与电子商务的全面整合,将"对话变成转换",从而创造一种独特的购物体验。

图 11.7　Payvment 功能

图 11.8　使用 Payvment 完成购物

Unit 11　Selling Products on Facebook: The Emergence of Social Commerce

图 11.9　ShopFans 应用

图 11.10　ShopFans 交易

当谈论到在脸书上购物时，消费者主要关心的问题之一就是隐私和安全。Adgregate Markets的CEO亨利·王解释道："Adgregate Markets的ShopFans是唯一由脸书的消费者安全软件独家供应商McAfee保证安全的社交商务解决方案，另外还有TRUSTe保证安全。这个方案允许电子零售商拥有一个自定义的脸书商店，由可以利用所有脸书社交渠道的McAfee和TRUSTe保障安全。"

ShopTab

当设置自己的脸书应用程序时，使用ShopTab（见图11.11）的商家可以从三个不同的定价选项（每500件商品10美元，每1,000件商品15美元或者每5,000件商品20美元）中选择，除了一个按月收取的会员费，并不需要签署长期合同，ShopTab也没有设置费用或任何比例的收益。当购物者准备从商家的ShopTab页面付款时，他们连接的是实际的商业网站，而不是直接通过脸书支付（见图11.12）。从脸书转移到商家网站的做法消除了顾客对任何延迟付款或违反安全的担忧，并且已经被证明会从超五亿脸书粉丝中产生惊人的网站流量。ShopTab凭借很低的月成本和简单的自我管理工具，成为商家加入脸书商务的一个非常棒的途径，并且几乎没有风险。ShopTab为每一个产品集成了脸书的社交共享功能，以帮助商家被其他脸书用户知晓。

让ShopTab引以为傲的是它同时方便了商家和顾客。ShopTab的联合创始人，杰伊·费特林格指出，低成本、顾客导向、通过谷歌基础平台上传产品数据源，以及为需要每天定价和库存更新的商家提供自动定时更新，这些优势使ShopTab成为行业的佼佼者。他解释说："我们花时间去了解客户想要怎样在脸书上和ShopTab交互，并确保可用性提供最好的体验。ShopTab也是第一个允许商家成批导入数据，以便立即发布产品价格和描述等信息，并载入产品图片的脸书电子商务应用程序，这样商家就不需要花费很多时间去上传每个产品图片了。"此外，ShopTab零售商也不用担心其他竞争对手的产品显示在他们的ShopTab里面，因为只有他们自己的产品才能显示在他们的脸书ShopTab上。

SocialShop

SocialShop的经营理念是把社交媒体和电子商务结合起来会吸引更多的客户，实现更多的销售。由Big Commerce创建的SocialShop提供五种项目，价格从24.95美元/月到299.95美元/月，再加上49.95美元开户费用。SocialShop易于使用，在社交环境下将商家与客户联系起来，它允许脸书用户在公司粉丝页上点击"商店"选项浏览产品，查看产品的照片，与朋友快速分享产品（见图11.13）。

Big Commerce联合创始人兼联合CEO米切尔·哈珀认为，易用性使得SocialShop从其他的脸书商务应用中脱颖而出（见图11.14）。他解释说："商家可以在不到两分钟的时间内将应用程序添加到脸书，并完整配置，以显示自己的产品。他们的粉丝不仅可以直接在脸书上浏览产品，还可以在他们的个人网页上分享这些产品。这是一个很好的病毒式营销形式。"

Unit 11　Selling Products on Facebook: The Emergence of Social Commerce

图 11.11　ShopTab 页面

图 11.12　支付页面跳转

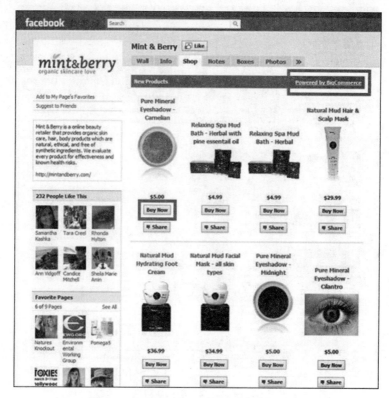

图 11.13 SocialShop 页面"商店"选项

图 11.14 SocialShop 页面

Unit 11　Selling Products on Facebook: The Emergence of Social Commerce

电子商务企业的脸书商务战略

一个成功的脸书商务战略的秘诀是想出有趣的方式，吸引你的受众并且为他们的购物体验增值。就像大部分的营销和销售渠道一样，没有一种方式能适合所有公司。因此，每个公司都需要一个独特的脸书商务战略，从而最大限度地使他们的"商店"标签成功。以下五个策略可以帮助你有效地吸引粉丝，并以正确的方式开展脸书商务。

确定你的粉丝群体的人口特征

每个脸书商务战略都应该是定制的，以迎合特定的脸书粉丝群的兴趣和偏好。Adgregate Markets的高级营销经理艾丽卡·特雷尔认为，对商家而言，在脸书上销售产品的关键是，"确定粉丝群的人口特征，并尝试根据他们的兴趣吸引他们。"通过准确地了解你是在和谁沟通，你将能够真正地与你的粉丝建立联系，从而创造一个成功的脸书商务营销活动。

关注消息推送

人们使用脸书是为了社交，看他们的朋友在做什么，看图片，而不是在脸书上购物。Milyoni战略和市场营销部的副总经理迪恩·阿尔姆斯解释说："（客户的）绝大多数的时间都花在看新闻推送上。脸书用户并不打算查找你的商店并购买你的产品，除非你通过消息推送吸引他们。"通过新闻推送吸引粉丝，这种方式可以包括任何能增加话题的内容，如发布有趣的状态更新、上传新照片或评论别人的页面等。

将粉丝变成传道士

在脸书上销售产品为商家提供了一个有趣的营销渠道，它将营销、销售和互动结合起来。ShopTab的首席执行官杰伊·弗特林格认为，当一个公司通过脸书商店积极吸引客户时，"粉丝们成为传道士，使用脸书来帮助传播有关你销售的产品的口碑。如果商家可以在人们谈论商品时就为他们开启购物流程，那么把消费者从知道商品变成实际购买所花费的时间和精力会减少"。

物质激励

Payvment的首席执行官克里斯蒂安·泰勒认为，"从你的脸书页面完成的独家交易和销售，可以带来巨大的利益和粉丝群体。"商家可以通过提供新产品首发销售、脸书专属优惠券和特价以及不良库存销售的渠道，来刺激产品在脸书上的销售。这些独有的推广方式是脸书商务病毒性营销的组成部分，是任何其他形式的广告无法比拟的。

变得透明

零售商们努力发展自己的脸书基地，并赢得粉丝的信任。既然社交媒体正在变得商业化，商家通过尊重他们的粉丝来维持粉丝们的信任是必要的。Big Commerce的联合创始人兼首席执行官米切尔·哈珀提醒商家，"关键是透明度，不要把脸书看作另一种'推销'你的客户的方式。相反，要把脸书看作和所有客户与发展前景建立透明关系的一种方式。"

脸书商务的未来

无论脸书商务如何的成功，必须记住，脸书是一个社交网站，而不是一个购物网站。迪恩·阿尔姆斯把脸书商务比作去看棒球比赛，"你在那里是为了享受球赛，但在比赛过程中，你很可能会购买一些食品、饮料，甚至可能是一顶球帽或一件T恤。但你并不是为了去那里'购买'。那些这样看待脸书角色的企业，与那些仅仅把脸书当成是另一种电子商务渠道的企业相比，在未来会做得更好。"

在这个早期阶段，目前还不清楚这种新的销售渠道在未来将如何演变和成长。杰伊·费特林格和米切尔·哈珀都认为，脸书的积分（脸书的虚拟货币）在未来的脸书商务中将扮演一个重要的角色，而艾丽卡·特雷尔预测，品牌营销战略将会有巨大变化。大家都同意，脸书商务将变革我们的购物方式，使其变成真正的社交体验。问题是，你的企业将如何利用这一激动人心的新机遇？

UNIT 12 What Do Consumers Really Want?

A. Advances in technology, logistics, payments and trust—coupled with increasing Internet and mobile access and consumer demand for convenience—have created a USD 1.9 trillion global online shopping arena, where millions of consumers no longer "go" shopping, but literally "are" shopping—at every moment and everywhere.

B. A recent report by KPMG International titled "Seeking customer centricity through omni business models", looked at how consumer and retail businesses are transforming to adapt to the shift from traditional shop-centric business models to a new world where the customer is increasingly at the center of a perpetual shopping experience. In this "customer-centric" reality, retailers need to be exceptionally sensitive and responsive to when and where their potential customers are making purchase decisions (both consciously and subconsciously) throughout their "always on" shopping journey.

C. The burning question is, how can consumer and retail companies achieve this nirvana of consumer mindreading? How can they identify and keep pace with the behaviors and preferences of customers today and tomorrow? How can they ensure their online strategy is acutely tailored to attract and win the diverse and dynamic customer segments they serve?

D. What 18,430 consumers told us during 2016, KPMG conducted an international study on consumer behaviors and preferences related to online shopping. The research was largely based on an online survey of 18,430 consumers living in more than 50 countries. The respondents were between the ages of 15 and 70, each having purchased at least one consumer product online in the past 12 months.

E. In addition to scrutinizing their online shopping behaviors, preferences, and decision processes, the study also explored consumers' plans for future online purchases, factors affecting trust and loyalty towards certain brands, and their sentiments and attitudes towards the companies that they do, or don't, choose to buy from.

F. The ultimate purpose of this research was to provide consumer goods and retail companies with the global and local insights into the specific behaviors and preferences of the customers they want to target. By understanding the uniqueness of different customer segments, companies can tailor their online strategies for maximum success.

G. The depth of the data collected for this study makes it possible for companies to analyze and forecast the behaviors and preferences of their customers by geography, generation (Millennials, Generation X or Baby Boomers) (see Fig. 12.1) or product category. The number of ways to filter and classify the data is too copious to summarize in a single report, so we will provide an overview of the global results, highlighting the most significant or interesting trends and comparisons among the major demographic groups and product categories.

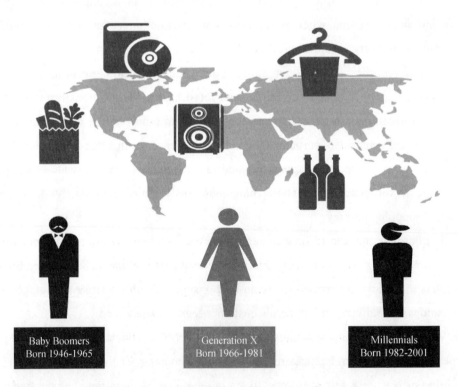

Fig. 12.1 Comparison Between Generations Generation

Unit 12 What Do Consumers Really Want?

Words and Expressions

arena [ə'rinə]	n.	竞技场；竞争舞台
onmibusiness ['ɒmnɪ'bɪznɪs]	n.	在线商务
responsive [rɪ'spɑːnsɪv]	adj.	敏感的，迅速积极反应的
nirvana [nɪə'vɑːnə]	n.	涅槃
dynamic [daɪ'næmɪk]	adj.	动态的；有活力的
scrutinize ['skruːtənaɪz]	v.	仔细查看
segment ['segmənt]	n.	部分
copious ['koʊpiəs]	adj.	大量的
highlight ['haɪˌlaɪt]	v.	强调；突出显示
demographic [ˌdemə'græfɪk]	adj.	人口统计学的；人口统计的

Questions

Directions: In this section, you are required to answer the following questions according to the information in the text.

(1) What do advances in technology, logistics, payments and trust lead to change in people's shopping?

(2) What is the feature of "customer-centric" shopping reality?

(3) Does the shopping shift make the relationship between buyers and retailers easier?

(4) What is the aim of international research conducted by KPMG?

(5) How does the research help the companies?

Exercises

Directions: In this section, there are five questions and for each of them there are four choices marked A, B, C and D. You should decide on the best choice.

(1) With the current advances, online shopping can be completed _____.

　　A. at home　　B. globally　　C. in a faraway place　　D. anywhere

(2) In the new shopping world, retailers should hold _____ attitude toward their customers.

　　A. attentive　　B. hostile　　C. differentiate　　D. random

(3) KPMG research studies many aspects of the online customers' shopping but _____.

　　A. their preferences to some brands

　　B. their trust of some brands

C. their feelings towards some brands

D. their capability of buying some brands

(4) Which of the following statement about the research is NOT true?

A. It can help the companies achieve maximum success.

B. It can develop the global and local insights into the customers' purchase.

C. It can help better understand the customer groups.

D. It can encourage the customers to purchase.

(5) Which of the following does not help to analyze and forecast the behaviors and preferences of their customers?

A. The location where the customers are living.

B. The time period when the customers are born.

C. The types of the customers prefer to purchase.

D. The necessity which the customers want.

Translation

消费者真正想要的是什么？

技术、物流、支付和信任方面的进步，加上互联网和移动接入的增加，以及消费者对便利性的需求，创造了一个价值1.9万亿美元的全球在线购物场所，数百万消费者不再"去"购物，而是随时随地"正在"购物。

最近，毕马威事务所发布了一份名为《通过全方位商务模式寻求客户中心性》的报告，该报告研究了消费者和零售企业如何转型，以适应从传统的以商店为中心的商务模式，转变为一个"客户逐渐变成永久购物体验的中心"的新世界。在这种"以客户为中心"的现实中，零售商需要对其潜在客户"一刻不停"的购物过程中做出购买决策（有意识和无意识地）的时间和地点非常敏感并快速响应。

亟待解决的问题是，消费者和零售企业如何才能实现对消费者读心的涅槃？他们如何能在现在和未来识别并跟上客户的行为和偏好？他们如何确保能够精心定制在线战略，以吸引并赢得他们所服务的多元化和充满活力的客户群体？

2016年，毕马威事务所开展了一项有关网上购物的消费者行为和偏好的国际研究，该研究主要基于对居住在50多个国家的18,430名消费者进行的在线调查。受访者年龄在15岁至70岁之间，且在过去12个月内至少在线购买了一种消费品。

除了仔细审查他们的在线购物行为、偏好和决策过程外，该研究还探讨了消费者未来在线购物的计划，影响信任和特定品牌忠诚度的因素，以及他们对于打算和不打算购买其产品的公司的情感和态度。

这项研究的最终目的是为消费品和零售公司提供关于全球和本地的目标客户的具体行为和偏好的见解。通过了解不同客户群体的独特性，公司可以定制其在线策略以获得最大成功。

本研究收集的数据有足够深度，所以公司可以按地理位置、一代人（千禧一代，X-代或婴儿潮一代）（见图12.1）或产品类别来分析和预测其客户的行为和偏好。过滤和分类数据的方法众多，无法在单个报告中进行总结，因此我们将概述全球结果，突出显示主要人口群体和产品类别中最重要或最有趣的趋势和比较。

图 12.1　代际比较

Chapter 5 E-Business Case Studies
第 5 篇 电子商务案例研究

- **UNIT 13**　Case Study of CRM: Securities Institute of Australia

- **UNIT 14**　Viral Marketing of Kettle Foods

Unit 13 Case Study of CRM: Securities Institute of Australia

A. Customer relationship management (CRM) systems are used by membership-based organizations, but not by many educational bodies. One Australian provider of higher education programs, the Securities Institute of Australia (SIA), a specialist in financial planning and related education courses, recently took the unusual step of buying and modifying an off-the-shelf CRM system to provide a range of functions including a student management system. Most other higher education providers in Australia purchase a student management system before considering the addition of CRM. The case study explains why the SIA took this innovative approach.

Background

B. The not-for-profit SIA is both an educational body and a membership-based organization in the finance industry. Apart from providing fee-for-service, customized and continuing professional development activities, the SIA offers a range of accredited courses ranging from Associate Diploma level to Masters Level, in programs such as the Diploma of Financial Advising and the Graduate Diploma in Financial Planning.

C. Over 28,500 subject enrollments were taken in 2000, with 40% of diploma subjects completed via distance education. The 2,000 enrollments included 1,200 international students from 59 different countries. The SIA has a joint venture with a Malaysian fund management organization and regularly delivers courses in Kuala Lumpur. The SIA has also secured a tender to provide an intensive training program in China in credit risk management.

D. SIA members in 2000 totaled 9,700 and included professionals in fields such as financial planning, superannuation and investment. The SIA has offices and teaching facilities in Sydney, its headquarters, Melbourne, Brisbane, Adelaide and Perth and its revenue in 2000 was USD 26.6 million.

CRM Business Drivers

E. Prior to the development of the CRM system, customer relationship management capabilities within the SIA were limited due to the lack of centralized information, lack of flexibility in its information systems and inadequate information analysis. CRM now provides an opportunity for the SIA to improve information handling, improve relationships with customers and reduce manual processes.

F. Another driver for the SIA is the threat from competitors. The threat is a reality for the SIA, as students in most countries of the world can easily enroll with organizations say, in the USA, which offer similar, specialized programs to the SIA and use online technologies extensively. The online revolution means that the SIA needs to match and surpass global competitors in its industry if it is to survive.

G. The CRM development at the SIA was also stimulated by the need to replace an aging technology infrastructure, the threat from competitors in the use of online communication with students and the desire to improve internal efficiencies. To address these and other issues, the SIA decided to purchase an existing CRM software package, Onyx, and to modify the software to suit the SIA, according to Information Technology Manager David Mitchell.

H. "We had a dire business need to replace the previous technological infrastructure: it was so bad it was threatening the business. Purchasing the CRM system was an opportunity to sweep away the old technology and to start again with a clean slate," Mr. Mitchell said.

I. Another driver for the initiative was the desire of the SIA to relate to its many distance education students in a more holistic way, offering them more than just a one-off course. It wanted to provide an enhanced range of one-to-one services to its students and members, rather than offer a restricted range of services for cohorts of students. According to General Manager, Business Development and Service, Dennis Macnamara the CRM approach enabled the SIA to relate to students as individuals, not as members of a class.

J. "The CRM system provides us with intelligence about each student or member and enables us to match each individual with value-added services. For instance, in an increasing number of our courses, a student can enroll at any time of the year, select what mix of distance education, online and face-to-face support is preferred, and communication between the two parties can continue for the rest of their career, not just for a semester," Dennis Macnamara said.

Description of the CRM System

K. The implementation of the CRM system involves three core parties: the SIA, the supplier of the CRM system Onyx and the website developer XT3. A team of up to eight staff from Onyx worked on the project from late 2000 to mid 2001, assisted by four SIA staff. Implementation of the Onyx Employee Portal (OEP) began as part of the first stage of the project in January 2001 with functionality rolled out progressively during first semester 2001. Onyx Customer Portal (OCP) development—in conjunction with SIA's revamped transactional website—began in June 2001, with a launch scheduled for August 2001. Functionality implemented in the first stage includes a central location to:

(1) access and manage information about students, practitioners, members and prospects;

(2) capture and maintain multiple addresses against each contact;

(3) capture and maintain multiple phone numbers against each contact;

(4) track demographic information (e.g., market sector and geographic region) against each customer;

(5) maintain one running tally of continuing professional development points against each individual;

(6) and provide systematic address validation and formatting.

L. A feature of the functioning CRM system is the easy-to-use web interface, which sits above the different databases in the SIA. The second phase of the project, in 2001, involves the implementation of the Customer Portal and the redevelopment of the website and the following functions.

(1) Customer portal functionality, lead capture and profiling.

(2) Commerce functionality, online product catalogue; order processing.

(3) Additional services, product registration; order history; profile management; online product and literature catalogue; web self-help; online service and support.

M. With the implementation of the second phase of the project completed in late 2001, a student is able to use the site to find out information about the SIA and its products. They can also search for a type of course to suit his/her needs, register interest to be notified about when an event might be available in their area, enroll in a course and a subject and apply for membership.

In addition they can find a program to suit his/her needs by answering a number of questions, e-mail an interesting part of the site to a friend, communicate with other students using a moderated web based forum, change their contact details and view their timetable and results.

N. Besides providing each user with the above services, the CRM system allows the SIA to secure the site; provide restricted and value-add content to designated or targeted SIA customers and promote its products and services and any news or success stories.

Challenges and Responses

O. The major challenges for the SIA in implementing the CRM system were not only to modify existing CRM software to suit the SIA's hybrid customer mix of students and members, but to understand how the system might impact on the SIA's business processes. It needed to alert staff to the impending changes on their jobs and help them develop new skills required to support the CRM system. Hence, a business process reengineering expert was engaged by the SIA to identify business processes that would be affected and to work with the staff. To ensure the CRM system is used optimally, internal policies also needed addressing.

P. According to David Mitchell, operational sections of the SIA needed to be alerted to what was going to happen with the implementation of the CRM system.

Q. Dennis Macnamara is conscious of the risks taken and the benefits that are possible.

R. "It was a brave decision by the SIA Board, as a CRM system normally sits on top of an existing system and doesn't drive it," he said.

S. "People don't yet realize how good it will be: it has huge potential. It breaks down the division in our business between students doing our accredited courses and our continuing professional development courses and our members. All of them can be serviced equally well, in a customized manner and more quickly with the CRM system. However, it is still early days and we have much more to do; we underestimated the amount of effort to get it right; and we still need to access infrastructure funds to make best use of it."

T. While the first two stages of the project will cost around USD 2.5 million, the SIA believes it chose the right path. There is now some potential for the SIA to sell its intellectual property in how it customized an off-the-shelf CRM product to suit its specific context.

U. Research by the SIA and their supplier suggests that the SIA's initiative, as an educational and membership body, in implementing a powerful CRM system as its main software engine, sitting atop the other software applications in the organization, is a world-class achievement.

Conclusion

V. The SIA case study shows a small, dynamic organization taking an innovative approach to integrating its back office and front office systems. The case study highlights the benefits of CRM when thoroughly planned and carefully implemented, in moving an organization to change its focus from supplying product to meeting customer demand.

Words and Expressions

securities [sɪ'kjʊrətiz]	n.	有价证券
accredit [ə'kredɪt]	vt.	授权,委任
superannuation [ˌsuːpərˌænju'eɪʃn]	n.	退休金
holistic [hoʊ'lɪstɪk]	adj.	整体的,全面的
revamp [ˌriː'væmp]	v.	修改,改进
demographic [ˌdemə'græfɪk]	adj.	人口统计学的
designate ['dezɪgneɪt]	v.	命名,指定
hybrid ['haɪbrɪd]	n.	杂交种,混合物
	adj.	混合的
impend [ɪm'pend]	vi.	(事件、危险等)逼近,即将发生
optimal ['ɒptɪməl]	adj.	最佳的

Questions

Directions: In this section, you are required to answer the following questions according to the information in the text.

(1) What are the CRM business drivers of SIA?
(2) What are the components of CRM system?
(3) How was the CRM system implemented?
(4) How to describe the CRM system?
(5) What is the major challenge for the SIA in implementing CRM system?

Exercises

Directions: In this section, you are going to read ten statements attached to the text. Each statement contains information given in one of the paragraphs in the text. Identify the paragraph from which the information is derived. You may choose a paragraph more than once.

(1) The CRM system can provide restricted and value-add content to assigned or targeted Securities Institute customers.

(2) SIA is both an educational body and a membership-based organization in the finance industry, which does not aim to make profits.

(3) We can learn that more focus on meeting its customer demand can help an organization to benefit more.

(4) Although the CRM system is helpful, people don't realize its huge potential.

(5) The need to take place of the old-fashioned technology infrastructure was also encouraged the development of the CRM.

(6) Customer relationship management capabilities within the SIA were limited owing to the absence of centralized information, lack of flexibility and inadequate information processing.

(7) The SIA, the supplier of the CRM system Onyx and the website developer XT3 are the three major components of the CRM system.

(8) Internal policies are necessary to ensure the CRM system is used as expected.

(9) The SIA believes it is the right choice despite the huge cost of the project.

(10) The web interface of the functioning CRM system is easy to use.

Translation

CRM 案例研究：澳大利亚证券协会

客户关系管理（CRM）系统被用于基于会员管理的组织中，但没有被很多教育机构使用。作为一个澳大利亚高等教育项目的提供者，澳大利亚证券协会（SIA）是财经计划及相关教育课程方面的专家，最近它采取了一个不寻常的举动：购买并优化了一套能提供包括学生管理系统功能在内的一系列功能的现成的CRM系统。澳大利亚大多数其他的高等教育提供者在考虑增加CRM之前都购买了学生管理系统。本案例研究解释了SIA为什么采取这一创新之举。

背　景

非营利性的SIA既是金融行业中的一个教育实体，又是一个基于会员管理的组织。除了提供付费服务、客户定制和持续的职业发展活动外，SIA还提供了一系列官方认证的课程，范围从大学预科文凭层次到硕士文凭层次，比如金融广告文凭以及财务规划硕士文凭。

在2000年，注册课程的人数超过了28,500，其中40%的文凭的课程完全通过远程教育实现。注册的2,000名学生中有1,200名是来自59个不同国家的国际学生。SIA与马来西亚基金管理组织有个共同的合资企业，并且定期在吉隆坡授课。SIA还在中国正式中标提供关于信用风险管理方面的集训课程。

在2000年SIA的成员已达9,700人，包括在一些诸如财务规划、退休金和投资等领域的专业人士。SIA在总部悉尼以及墨尔本、布里斯班、阿德莱德、珀斯设有办事处和教学机构，2000年它的总收入为2,660万美元。

CRM 商业动力

在CRM系统开发前，由于信息系统缺乏集中的信息、弹性以及信息分析不足，SIA的客户关系管理能力受到限制。CRM现在为SIA提供了用来改进其信息处理能力、改善其与客户关系和减少人工流程的机会。

SIA的另一个动力来自竞争对手的威胁。威胁对于SIA而言是实实在在存在的,因为世界上大多数国家的学生能很容易地在一个教育机构注册,比如美国,它提供与SIA相似的专业项目,并广泛使用在线技术。在线革命意味着SIA要想生存下去,就要与本行业的全球竞争对手保持相当,或超越他们。

SIA的CRM发展也来自更换过时的技术设施的需求的刺激,来自学生应用在线交流沟通的竞争对手的威胁以及提高内部效率的愿望。为了解决这些和其他问题,SIA决定购买现成的CRM套装软件包——Onyx,据信息技术主管大卫·米歇尔称,他们对该程序进行了修改,使之适合SIA的需求。

米歇尔先生说:"我们有一个强烈的商业需求去更换先前的技术设施——它太糟糕了,以至于对业务产生了威胁。购买CRM系统是清除陈旧技术并重新开始的机会。"

另一个动力则是来自SIA希望以一种更加全面的方式与那些接受远程教育的学生进行联系,而不仅仅是向他们提供一次性的课程。它想要给学生和会员提供更大范围的一对一的服务,而不是给一大批学生提供一个有限范围的服务。按照业务发展与服务总经理丹尼斯·麦克纳马拉的说法,CRM使SIA把学生作为个体进行联系,而不是作为班级的一个成员。

丹尼斯·麦克纳马拉说:"CRM系统提供给我们每一个学生或会员的信息,使我们能够给每一个个体提供增值服务,比如,在数量不断增加的课程中,一个学生可以在一年的任何时候注册上课,选择任意组合的远程教育,在线和面对面的支持成为首选。双方的交流可以在其整个职业生涯持续而不仅是一个学期。"

CRM 系统的描述

CRM系统的实施包含3个主要参与者:SIA、CRM系统Onyx提供者和网站开发商XT3。从2000年年底至2001年年中,来自Onyx的8人工作小组在证券学院4名工作人员的帮助下从事此项工作。在2001年1月,Onyx雇员门户(OEP)作为该项目第一阶段的一个部分开始实施,并在2001年第一学期逐步推出。按照一份2001年8月的启动计划,Onyx客户门户(OCP)的开发与修改后的SIA交易网站的对接于2001年6月展开,并计划于2001年8月试开通。第一阶段实施的功能包含的核心是:

(1)获得并管理有关学生、从业者、会员和可能的候选人(潜在顾客)的信息;
(2)针对每一次联络获取和维护多重地址;
(3)针对每一次联络获取和维护多个电话号码;
(4)针对每一个顾客,追踪人口统计学信息(例如细分市场和地理区域);
(5)针对每一个人,保持一个连续职业发展的动态记录;
(6)提供系统化的地址确认和格式编排。

CRM系统的一个特征是基于SIA的不同数据库基础之上的易于使用的网络界面。在2001年，项目的第二阶段包含顾客门户实施和网站再开发及以下功能：

（1）客户门户功能，线索获取和存档；

（2）交易功能，在线产品目录、订单处理；

（3）附加服务，产品注册、订单历史记录、用户画像管理、在线产品和文献目录、网页自助及在线服务支持。

项目第二阶段在2001年后期完工，学生能够利用站点查找SIA及其产品信息。他们还可以查找适合他们需求的课程类型，登记其兴趣，以便当有其感兴趣的事件发生时可以接到通知；注册课程及科目并申请加入会员。除此之外，他们还能通过回答一系列问题找到适合他们需求的项目，并将该网站有趣的部分通过E-mail发送给朋友；使用成熟的网络论坛与其他学生进行交流；改变他们的联系信息并浏览他们的课表和成绩。

除了给每一个使用者提供以上服务外，CRM系统还允许SIA维护网站安全；提供严格限定的增值内容给指定客户或者目标客户以促销产品和服务，并提供一些新闻和成功的例子。

挑战和回应

在实施CRM系统时，SIA最主要的挑战不仅仅是需要修改现存的CRM软件以适应SIA学生和会员组成的混合客户群体，而且还需要了解该系统如何影响SIA的业务流程。这需要提醒员工关注他们工作上即将发生的变化，以及培养他们使用CRM系统的新技能。所以SIA聘请了业务流程重组专家来分析可能受影响的业务流程，并与员工共事。为了确保CRM系统得到最佳使用，内部的政策也需要调整。

大卫·米歇尔先生认为，应该提醒SIA的运营部门伴随CRM系统的实施将会发生的事情。

丹尼斯·麦克纳马拉意识到实施CRM系统所带来的风险和可能的收益。

他说："SIA董事会做出了一个勇敢的决定，因为CRM系统通常是位于现有系统尖端之上的，而不是（在底层）驱动它们。"

"人们还没有认识到它会带来什么样的好处：它拥有巨大的潜力。它打破了学习我们的认证课程及继续职业发展课程的学生和会员之间的业务分隔。借助于CRM系统，他们所有人都能作为客户并以定制方式更加快捷而平等地享受良好的服务。然而，现在只是处在早期，我们需要做的事情还很多，我们低估了取得成果所要付出的努力，我们还需要去争取基础设施资金，以实现这一系统的最佳利用。"

尽管项目的前两个阶段将耗资250万美元，SIA相信自己的选择是正确的。现在SIA拥有销售知识产权的潜力，也就是如何将现成的CRM套装软件定制成适应自己具体环境的应用。

SIA及其供应商所做的研究表明，SIA作为一个教育机构和一个会员制机构，实施强大的CRM系统，并成为位于其他软件应用之上的软件引擎，是世界级的成就。

结　论

SIA案例研究展示了一个小型的、充满活力的组织，这个组织采用创新的方法来整合它的前台与后台办公系统。案例研究强调了详细规划和认真实施CRM系统时，通过促使一个组织从提供产品转向满足客户需求过程中能获得的收益。

UNIT 14 — Viral Marketing of Kettle Foods

Overview

A. So, do you want to make a difference in the world? You say you want to start a business revolution? That is exactly what Kettle Foods did with their latest e-marketing campaign. The company gave the general public and its loyal fans a chance to name the next Kettle chip flavor. Yes, you actually had the chance to create the flavor "Strawberry Cream". Thankfully, our faith in the voting public was restored when "Cheddar Beer" and "Spicy Thai" were chosen, but that's another story. Kettle leveraged its super-loyal base of customers to get momentum. The campaign then spread nationally via media outlets, word of mouth, and achieved strong results for Kettle by growing its loyal list of customers and increasing brand awareness.

B. The Kettle Foods "Crave" e-marketing campaign is outlined in the following case study. Overall, the study focuses on the planning stage of a successful campaign through to the results stage. The case study is meant to inform you on what it takes to create a successful e-marketing and viral campaign. It draws in aspects of word of mouth, word of mouse, and pre-existing marketing practices.

Step 1: Strategic Planning

C. All e-mails created for an e-marketing campaign and sent to a list of prospects or customers should be backed by a strategic plan. The Kettle strategic plan was in the form of a project brief written by Kettle's PR agency, Maxwell PR. The plan included a creative online customer interaction piece to be developed by eROI. This case study outlines the business and marketing strategies for the e-marketing campaign, as well as the intended creative approach to meet those objectives. The project briefs included a scope of work and resources required, as well as timeline and budget.

D. While each company has a different set of objectives and requirements, there are commonalities in both strategy and tactical execution. The objective for Kettle was quite simple: develop a new and exciting chip flavor to add to their current 20 flavor offering. The new flavor needed to be as unique as Kettle itself. Can you say "Spicy Thai"? Kettle capitalized on its strong brand equity and was able to step outside the box on flavor and its approach in naming the new flavor. Have you ever been asked by another company to help choose an aspect of its next product?

Step 2: Driving Momentum and List Management

E. It's necessary to start with a solid foundation to build a larger structure. List procurement for this campaign was just the beginning. Oregon-based Kettle Foods seeded their option list by setting up booths in many trade shows in both Washington and Oregon. Where better than your own backyard to start generating buzz about a new offering? During the trade shows, Kettle asked attendees of all ages to come up with a new flavor they would like to see Kettle produce as their next chip flavor. The information was passed along to Maxwell PR and then uploaded to Kettle's eROI account. The goal of the e-marketing campaign was to learn as much as possible about the customer or prospect.

F. The focus of the campaign was to foster the emotional connection with the Kettle brand in a way that customers were co-creating and owning a part of the company by naming a chip flavor. Ultimately, Kettle was able to accomplish this and grow its potential consumer base and build brand awareness. The important metrics were the Kettle Crave site's Send-to-a-Friend function and the web Sign-up form. The viral nature of this campaign drove customers to Kettle's site and encouraged them to subscribe to Kettle's e-mail list. Additionally, Kettle set two more measurable goals of a 25% read rate and a 5% click—through rate on its e-newsletter to launch the campaign. Both were very obtainable given the list quality, PR and creative involved with this campaign.

G. In order to engage and retain the customer's attention, Kettle and Maxwell PR collaborated with eROI to create the "Crave-O-Meter™". This piece was the most engaging element of the campaign. The Crave-O-Meter™ enabled the customer to be a part of the Kettle brand, and generated options for further contact and brand awareness (see Fig. 14.1). As the online chip voters moused over the Crave-O-Meter™, they were greeted with "*<1> I'll try anything once, except this*" to middle-of-the-road "*<3> I'm on the fence*" to the ecstatic "*<5> This sounds delicious! I could eat an entire bag*".

Fig. 14.1   Crave-O-Meter™ Options

H. One of the primary purposes of this campaign, like most campaigns, was to grow list size and list quality. The secondary purpose was to grow brand awareness over a larger demographic, extending from the Northwest to the rest of the country. The objective and vehicle to achieve these goals was the Crave-O-Meter™ to develop a new chip flavor.

I. Kettle's call to action resonates throughout the campaign; all actions are tied back to the Crave-O-Meter™. This is the driving force for customer communication. The goal is to drive the customer from the e-mail back to Kettle's website where they rate their taste buds. It is easily passed on to others, making e-mail growth quite efficient.

J. The Kettle campaign scored with its list management and list growth capabilities. Imagine the ability to grow your list from 5,000 e-mails to 15,000 quality e-mails in less than 10 weeks.

K. Every person voted on each of the 5 flavors for a cumulative total of 40,000 votes. The original list was generated by direct contact with consumers and potential consumers. The growth of the list happened organically and took off virally through word of mouth and word of mouse. This type of marketing yielded excellent results. The Crave-O-Meter™ was the key viral component of the campaign by driving users to the website and then having them add themselves to the e-mail list.

L. Results：

(1) 4,000 votes in first week；

(2) Taste test on "Good Morning America"；

(3) Interest by "Ellen Degeneres Show"；

(4) Over 40,000 votes cast by the end of a 10 week campaign.

Fig. 14.2 is the results of votes.

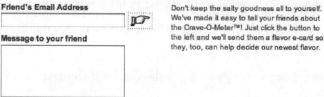

Fig. 14.2 The Results of Votes

Step 3: E-mail Creative and Production

M. In order to create an e-mail that will generate a response, we must first analyze its elements, the most important of which include:

From

This is the sender's name and e-mail, in this case "Kettle Foods" and "thedirt@kettlefoods.com". By using this e-mail address and e-newsletter name "The Dirt", Kettle created a brand within a brand. In effect, the company created a "Trusted Sender". Now, the recipient has a better chance of recognizing the sender and responding to a more engaging e-mail.

Subject

The "subject" line is perhaps one of the most critical components of any e mail campaign. Kettle took the approach of inviting the potential consumer to be a part of the Kettle family. The company maintained a concise, relevant subject line, "The Dirt—January 2005". It is descriptive, memorable, and true to the Kettle brand.

Personalization

Kettle highlighted personal names of its customers who submitted the 5 initial flavors to be voted on. While a personalized greeting can be an important element in an e-mail, Kettle did not use a salutation in its launch of "The Dirt".

Body Copy

The format chosen by Kettle is one that stretches across its brand. Kettle spent time and space to highlight not only their chips, but also their brand. The company is creating more awareness as the consumer transfers from the e-mail to Kettle's landing page.

Graphical Elements—HTML Only

A picture is worth a thousand words, and Kettle wanted to make sure to convey the correct 1,000 words. The company chose graphical elements that truly focus on its grassroots brand and who they are as a company.

Offer

Things must be placed in a logical order. Having the e-mail lead off with a value proposition or "grabber" is a great way to start out. Consider this: you are helping decide the flavor of the next chips Kettle will introduce to the world. How many people can say they helped choose a product for a major corporation? This leads us into our call to action.

Call to Action—Hyperlinks, Buttons

What do you want your customer to do? In this e-mail campaign, the call to action was to visit www.crave.kettlefoods.com and vote online for the 5 potential chip flavors. At a larger level, the implied call to action was to help be a part of the next big thing. Lastly, once you've gone through this authentic, unique, and fun online experience, you can tell your friends about how you just voted for "Cheddar Beer" as the next flavor of chips from Kettle and they should, too.

Step 4: E-mail Launch and Campaign Management

N. Carefully timed follow-up e-mails provide an additional reminder to the respondents and serve to keep the brand in the consumer's mind.

O. Media outlet measurement is focused and driven to the Kettle Foods landing page (see Fig. 14.3). This was charted by a 24% increase in newsletter signups, an increase of 1,000 new names a month.

Fig. 14.3　Kettle Foods Landing Page

P. Campaign management takes many factors into account, such as the day to send your message off, the time the e-mail will go out, how to test multiple messages and designs, and the platform you are going to use to send your e-mails off. In the world of e-mail, you only have moments to react and when you send a message erroneously, you can't stop it or take it back. If you are sure everything is in the right place and all the pieces fit, send a test off first.

Step 5: Distribution and Tracking

Q. The e-mail statistics within eROI's platform show a 30% read rate and a 5.4% click through rate on the first e-mail campaign (see Fig. 14.4).

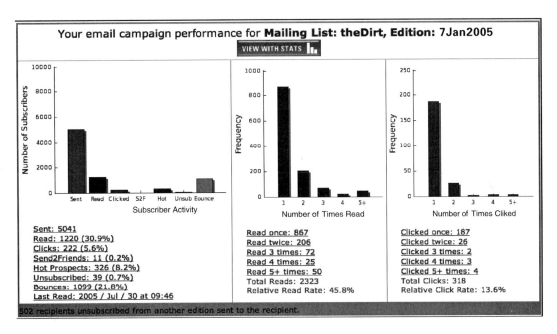

Fig. 14.4 The E-Mail Statistics Result

R. Not only could Kettle push personalized data to a website from the eROI platform, but Kettle could also pull it from www.crave.kettlefoods.com through a lead capture form and back into the e-mail tracking platform (see Fig. 14.5). This brings us full circle. The campaign leveraged a strong brand and garnered solid, trackable results.

S. Tracking individual customer behavior through the entire site was a much needed aspect of the campaign. Kettle learned more about the customer's perceptions and behavior and how those reflected on its brand. Ultimately, Kettle learned what products worked and which products were missing.

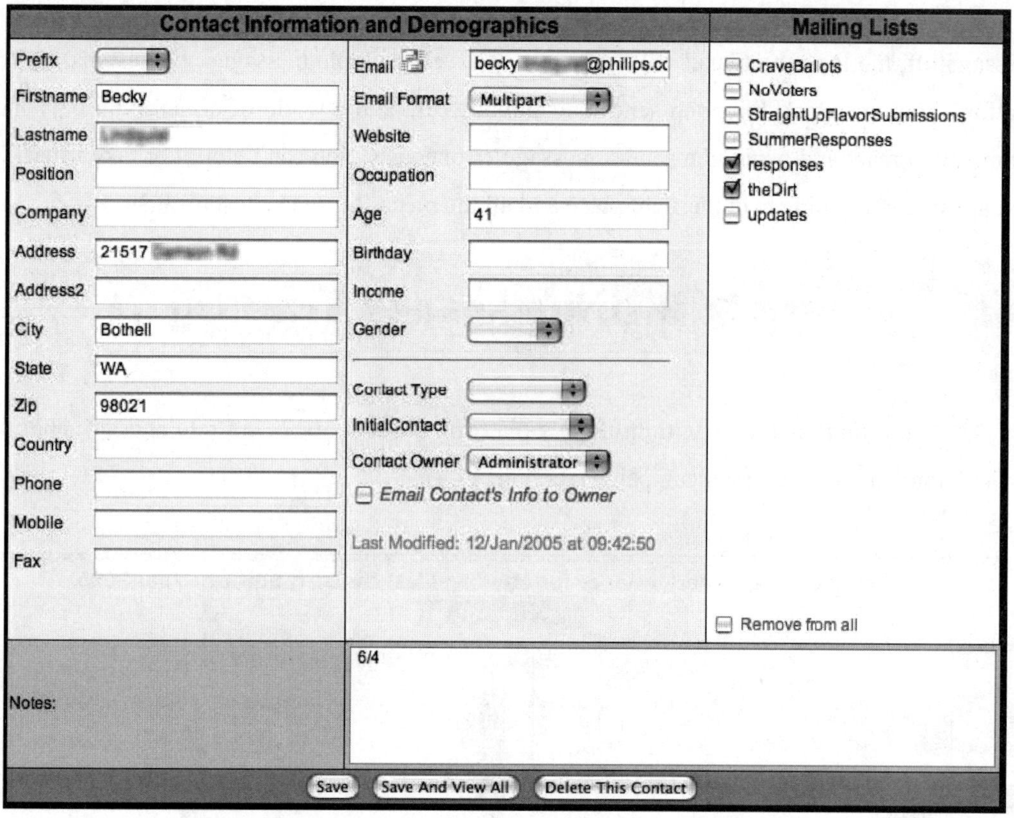

Fig. 14.5　The E-mail Tracking Platform

Step 6: Reporting and Analysis

T. The reporting was the reason Kettle embarked on this strange trip to begin with. What are the results? We did all this work, now show us the money, and that is what Kettle got.

(1) List growth to the tune of 1,000 new names per week.

(2) Brand Awareness—50,000 votes and campaign received national media attention in the form of TV ("Good Morning America" and interest from the "Ellen Degeneres Show"), newspapers (*Portland Business Journal*), and radio (OPB).

(3) Useful consumer data obtained—individual customer/prospect behavior tracked from e-mail and throughout the entire micro-site.

U. The next step for Kettle is to take the results and move to the analysis phase to create their next campaign. The company will look at what works, what people want, and what drives new customers to their site.

Unit 14　Viral Marketing of Kettle Foods

V. Take a look at the current campaign on the website, which continues to evolve and foster creativity with its customer base.

W. So what are you waiting for? Start working on your new viral campaign today and see what kind of business you can start. With proper planning and a strong message, you too will be successful.

Words and Expressions

viral ['vaɪrəl]	adj.	病毒性的
momentum [moʊ'mentəm]	n.	势头，动量
equity ['ekwəti]	n.	资产净值
tactical ['tæktɪkl]	adj.	战术上的
capitalize on		利用
vehicle ['viːəkl]	n.	机动车辆，媒介
resonate ['rezəneɪt]	vt.	共振，（对某人）有重要性
cumulative ['kjuːmjəleɪtɪv]	adj.	累积的
hyperlink ['haɪpərlɪŋk]	n.	超文本链接

Questions

Directions: In this section, you are required to answer the following questions according to the information in the text.

(1) How did Kettle use the Internet to grow its list?
(2) How did Kettle design the e-mail sent to the customer list?
(3) What elements should a creative e-mail cover?
(4) What did Kettle get from the e-mail campaign?
(5) What can we learn from this case?

Exercises

Directions: In this section, you are required to answer the questions with T or F.
T (for True) if the statement agrees with the information given in the passage;
F (for False) if the statement contradicts the information given in the passage.

(1) Kettle Foods started a business revolution with their e-marketing campaign.
(2) The Kettle strategic plan included a creative face-to-face customer interaction piece.

(3) Each company has different set of objectives and requirements, and there will not be commonalities in strategy and tactical execution.

(4) The purpose of the e-marketing campaign was to know as much as possible about the customer or prospect.

(5) One of the basic purposes of the campaign was to increase list size and list quality.

(6) Kettle's campaign aims to drive the customer form the e-mail back to Kettle's website where they evaluate their taste buds, which is not easily passed on to others.

(7) The Kettle campaign won its reputation with list management and list growth capabilities.

(8) The growth of the list happened organically and took off virally through word of mouth and the use of Internet.

(9) A personalized greeting is an important element, so Kettle use a salutation in an e-mail.

(10) Keeping track on individual customer behavior through the entire site was a much needed aspect of the campaign.

Translation

克特食品的病毒式营销

概 述

嗯,你想要改变这个世界吗?你说你想要开始一次商业变革?这正是克特食品最新的电子市场营销活动所做的。该公司为公众及其忠实客户提供为下一种克特薯片口味命名的机会。是的,你确实有机会创造"草莓奶油"口味。让人欣慰的是,当"切达啤酒"和"泰国辛辣"口味被选中的时候,我们对公众投票这一决策又恢复了信心。不过,那是另一个故事。克特以其超级忠诚的客户基础为杠杆,获得了强劲的发展势头。这项活动随后通过媒体渠道及人们的口头宣传,迅速在全国扩散开来,为克特赢得了更多的忠诚客户,并提高了品牌知名度,取得了丰硕的成果。

克特食品"渴望"电子市场营销活动可在以下案例研究中概述。总体而言,本研究的重点在于一次成功的宣传活动的规划阶段到结果阶段。案例研究的目的是要告诉你如何去创建一个成功的电子市场营销和病毒式活动。本文从口头宣传、网络宣传以及原有的销售活动等方面加以描绘。

第1步:战略规划

为进行电子市场营销活动所创造的并发送给潜在客户或客户的所有电子邮件都应该有战略规划的支持。克特战略规划以项目摘要的形式由克特的公关机构——麦克斯韦公关公司完成。这项计划包含一个由eROI公司开发的有创意的网上客户互动板块。这个案例研究概述了此次电子市场营销活动的业务及营销策略,以及实现这些目标的创造性方法。本项目摘要包括工作范围和所需资源,以及时间表和预算。

虽然每家公司都有一套不同的目标和要求,但在战略和战术执行上还是有共同点的。克特的目标很简单:开发一种新的令人兴奋的口味并添加到目前已存在的20个薯片口味中,新口味必须像克特本身一样独特。你能建议"泰国辛辣口味"吗?克特凭借其强大的品牌资产,有能力通过命名新口味的方法一步跳出传统风味的限制。你曾经被其他公司要求帮助其选择下一个产品的一个方面吗?

第2步：驱动要素和列表管理

要建设更大的机构，就要有坚实的基础。清单采购仅仅是这项运动的开始。位于俄勒冈州的克特食品通过在华盛顿和俄勒冈州的许多商展中设置摊位而获得下拉菜单式问卷表格。还有哪里会比在自己的地盘上发行一种新的产品更合适呢？在商展过程中，克特要求在场的各个年龄段的人群提出他们希望克特生产的下一种薯片的口味。这些信息传递给麦克斯韦公关公司，然后上传到克特公司的eROI账户。电子市场营销活动的目标是尽可能多地了解顾客或潜在顾客。

本次活动的重点是要通过对新口味命名，使顾客共同创建和拥有公司的一部分，来培养顾客与克特品牌的情感联系。最终，克特做到了这一点，并扩大其潜在客户基础，建立品牌知名度。克特的最重要的策略是在Crave网站提供了"发送给朋友"的功能与"会员注册表"。这项运动的病毒式特性驱使顾客浏览克特的网站，并鼓励他们订阅克特的电子邮件列表。此外，克特设置了两个可衡量的目标——25%的阅读率和5%的点击率，作为发起这项活动的条件。考虑到本次活动的名单质量、公共关系和创意，这两个目标是非常容易实现的。

为了引起顾客并保持的注意，克特和麦克斯韦公关公司与eROI合作，创立了"Crave-O-Meter™"商标。这是这项活动最有吸引力的部分。"Crave-O-Meter™"，使顾客成为克特的一部分，并产生进一步接触和品牌认知的选项（见图14.1）。当在线投票人的鼠标掠过"Crave-O-Meter™"的时候，映入他们眼帘的是："〈1〉任何东西我都可以尝试一下，除了这个"，代表中间立场的"〈3〉我犹豫不决"，代表狂热爱好者的"〈5〉这听起来真好吃！我可以吃一整袋"。

同大多数的活动一样，这次活动的主要目标之一，就是增加列表的规模和质量。第二个目标是通过从西北地区扩展到本国其他地区，在更大的地域范围内扩大品牌的知名度。这一活动的目标和实现这些目标的方法是利用"Crave-O-Meter™"来开发新口味。

克特的呼吁行动在整个活动引起共鸣；一切行动都与"Crave-O-Meter™"相关。这样做的目的是让客户从电子邮件回到Kettle网站，在Kettle网站上对自己的口味进行评价。这样就很容易把评价的信息传递给其他人，并使电子邮件的数量高效地增长。

克特营销活动中的列表管理和名单增长能力受到赞赏。可以想象一下这种能力，在不到10周的时间里，客户的名单从5,000个电子邮件增加到15,000个高质量的电子邮件。

每个人对这5种口味进行投票，数量累计多达4万张。原来的列表是由直接接触消费者和潜在的消费者产生的。通过口头上的宣传和网上宣传，名单以病毒式增长，发生质的飞跃。这种类型的市场营销取得了很好的效果。"Crave-O-Meter™"是这次病毒式营销的关键组成部分，它驱动用户访问克特网站，并将自己加入电子邮件列表中。

Unit 14 Viral Marketing of Kettle Foods

图14.1 CRAVE-O-METER™选项

结果：

（1）第一周共4,000票；

（2）《早安美国》的口味测试；

（3）引发了《艾伦·德杰尼勒斯脱口秀》的关注；

（4）第10周周末已超过40,000票。

图14.2为投票结果。

图14.2 投票结果

第3步：电子邮件创作与生产

为了创建一个有回应的电子邮件，我们必须先分析其元素，其中最重要的元素如下。

发件人

这是发件人的姓名和电子邮件。在该例中为"克特食品"和"thedirt@kettlefoods.com"。用该邮件地址和取名为"The Dirt"的电子通信，克特创造了品牌中的品牌。实际上，该公司设立了"可信赖寄件人"。现在，收件人有更好的机会识别出该寄件人，并回复更有吸引力的邮件。

主题

"主题"是所有邮件营销活动中最重要的组成部分之一。克特采取的做法是邀请潜在消费者成为克特大家庭中的一部分。该公司采用简明扼要的主题，即"The Dirt——2005年1月"。它具有描述性，让人过目难忘，这是克特品牌的真实写照。

个性化

克特突出显示最初提出5种口味进行投票的顾客的名字。虽然个性化的问候在一封电子邮件中可以发挥重要作用，但克特在其发布的"The Dirt"中未使用问候语。

邮件主体

克特食品选择的格式在品牌范围内是统一的，克特花了很多时间和精力来突出它们的薯片产品以及品牌。当消费者从邮件转移到公司的登录页面时，公司就可以建立起更高的知名度。

图形元素——只有网页

一幅图片胜过千言万语，而克特希望能借助图片正确传达那些通常需要上千文字表达的信息。克特公司选择将切实的重点放在能够表达其基本品牌以及公司定位的图形元素上。

提议

事情一定要有一个逻辑顺序。在电子邮件中以价值主张或"抓手"开头是一个很好的方式。试想：你正在帮助克特决定将要面世的下一种薯片的口味。有多少人可以说他们曾帮助大公司选择产品？这种想法将成为我们的动力。

呼吁行动——超链接，按钮

你希望你的客户做什么？在这个电子邮件营销活动中，呼吁的是访问www.crave.kettlefoods.com，并为5种可能的口味进行在线投票。在更大的层面上，隐含的行为号召是为了帮助其成为下个大事件的一部分。最后，一旦你经历了这次真实的、独一无二的、有趣的在线经历，你就可以告诉你的朋友你是怎么把切达啤酒口味选为克特的下一种口味的，并告诉他们，他们也应该这样做。

第 4 步：电子邮件活动启动及商业活动管理

定时向受访者发送后续邮件，可以提供额外的提醒，有助于消费者记住该品牌。

媒体渠道评价的重点集中在克特食品的登录页（见图14.3）。新闻组订阅量每月增长24%，每月增加1,000个用户。

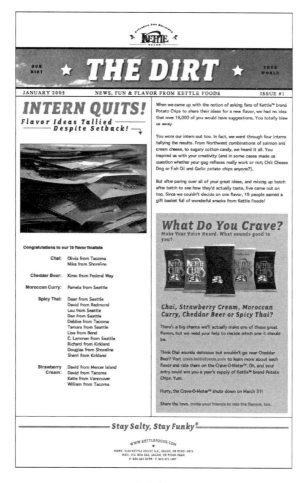

图14.3　克特食品登录页面

商业活动管理要考虑多方面的因素，如发送信息的日期、发送电子邮件的时间、测试各种信息和设计方案的方法，以及发送电子邮件的平台。在电子邮件的世界里，你只有瞬间的时间做出反应，而且当你错误地发送信息的时候，你无法阻止它或收回它。如果你确信每个细节都是准确的，那么首先应发出一封测试邮件。

第5步：分配和跟踪

eROI电子邮件平台的统计数据显示，在首次电子邮件活动中有30%的阅读率和5.4%的点击率（见图14.4）。

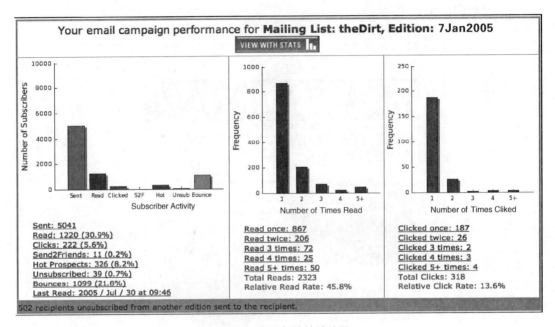

图14.4　电子邮件统计结果

克特不仅能从eROI电子邮件平台推送个性化数据到一个网站，而且可以通过捕获表格的形式把它从www.crave.kettlefoods.com返回到电子邮件跟踪平台（见图14.5）。这带给我们一个完整的循环。该活动以强势品牌为杠杆，获得了坚实的、可跟踪的结果。

在整个网站中追踪个别客户的行为是这项商业活动的一个非常必要的方面。克特更多地了解了客户的观念和行为，以及如何将这些反映到自己的品牌中。最终，克特了解到什么样的产品能达到预期的效果以及哪些产品将要下架。

第6步：报告和分析

这份报告是克特开始这一神奇的活动的原因。结果如何？我们做了一切的努力，现在我们看到了效益，这是克特所得到的：

（1）列表名单增长速度高达1,000名/周；

（2）品牌知名度——获得5万投票并且该活动得到全国媒体的关注，包括电视（《早安美国》，《艾伦·德杰尼勒斯脱口秀》的关注）、刊物（《波特兰商业杂志》）以及无线电台（OPB）等形式；

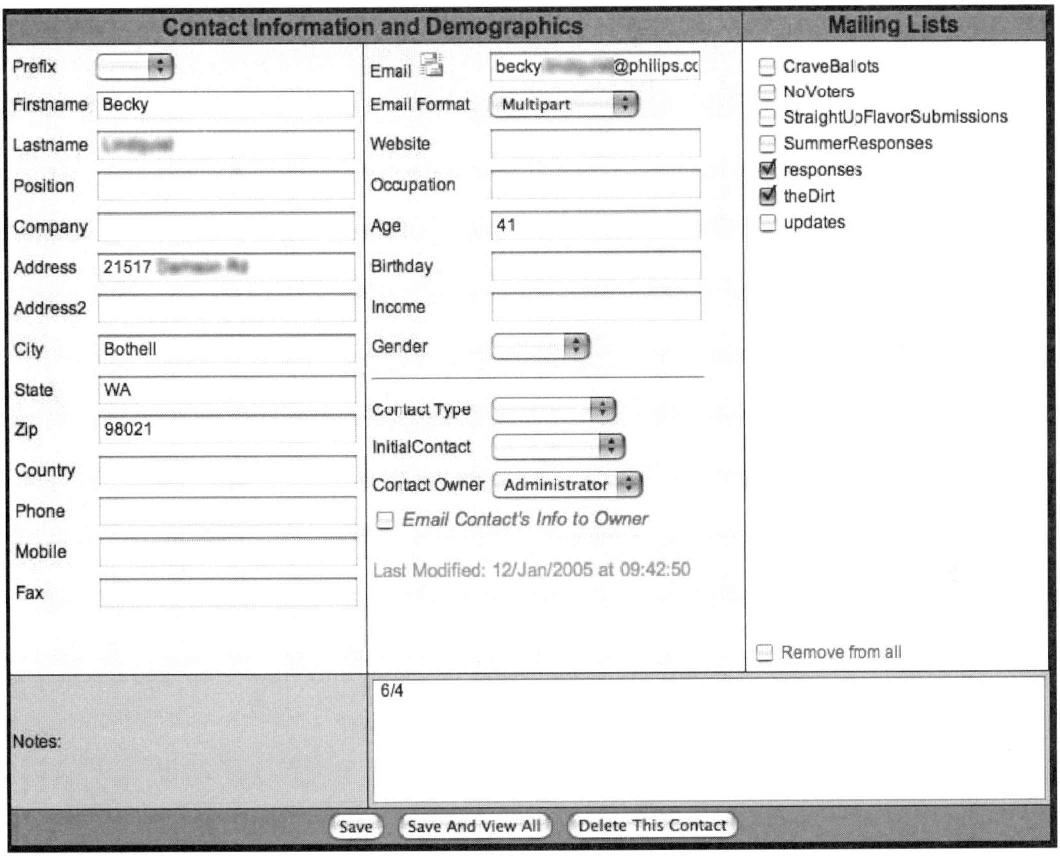

图14.5　电子邮件跟踪平台

（3）消费者的有效资料——从电子邮件到整个微型网站的个别顾客／潜在客户行为跟踪。

克特下一步要采集结果并进入分析阶段，以创建它们的下一次商业活动。该公司将考虑如何达到预期效果，人们想要什么，以及怎样促使新客户进入其网页。

可以去网站看一下当前的商业活动，它们会继续发展，并以客户为基础培养创造力。

所以，你还在等什么呢？今天就开启你的新病毒式商业活动，看看你可以启动什么样的业务。凭借适当的规划和作用强大的信息，你也一定能取得成功。

Chapter 6 E-Business Technology and Security Issues
第 6 篇 电子商务技术与安全

- UNIT 15　Some Technology Trends Affecting E-Business
- UNIT 16　E-Business Relies on Security
- UNIT 17　UNCTAD B2C E-Commerce Index 2017

UNIT 15 Some Technology Trends Affecting E-Business

TEXT

A. Without aiming to provide exhaustive or comprehensive coverage of the issues, the following pages will address some aspects of technology use that have been particularly prominent in the e-business arena and that will probably influence the development of e-business in coming years.

The Growth of Broadband

B. The spread of broadband Internet access and related technologies is one reason for Internet traffic rapid growth. The spread of broadband is not only enabling existing Internet users to exchange information more easily, it is also attracting new users. Some operators report that 30 to 50 percent of their new broadband subscribers have never had an Internet subscription before.

C. Broadband availability has grown very fast in the past two years. Two dominant technologies have an almost equal share of the world broadband market: digital subscriber line (DSL), with 50 percent, and cable, with 45 percent. How will the widespread adoption of broadband influence businesses? Fast Internet access is the main reason for subscribers to switch to broadband technologies. Because data flow faster and users waste much less time waiting for web pages to download, and because their connections are always on, broadband adopters tend to spend significantly more time online. At the same time, consumers will be able to seek more information, compare more options, or sample digital products.

D. With regard to broadband's influence on the organization of enterprises or on transactions between businesses, although a number of initiatives aim at building new business models around broadband, no application of it has emerged with an impact on the functioning of markets or on the management of companies that is substantially different from the effects of earlier commercial applications of the Internet. This is not to say that broadband will have no impact on businesses. Businesses buy much more online content than consumers, and broadband makes such content more accessible, easier to use, and therefore more sellable, especially to small and medium-size enterprises (SMEs). Broadband allows several users to share an Internet connection, which can reduce the cost of every individual connection, an important consideration for SMEs. For larger enterprises, the ability to centralize data and applications in a single storage facility while enabling many users in distant locations to access and use sizeable amounts of information may facilitate the adoption of new forms of organization. Other, broader effects on the economy can also be envisioned. Besides improving access to information society services (e.g. e-health, e-education, e-government) that have indirect but real effects on the productivity of an economy, broadband adoption, like any major new technology, can encourage innovation and thus stimulate economic growth.

Security Issues

E. A secure environment is not any more essential for e-business than it is for business in the physical world. Every commercial transaction involves a risk with which participants are normally familiar enough to judge whether the expected returns justify accepting the uncertainty of a potential loss. Even in the presence of considerable risk, if the expected returns are sufficiently high, someone will be willing to take that risk. As e-business becomes part of the everyday experience of the majority of people, who tend to be more risk-averse than early adopters of technology, security in all its dimensions becomes crucially important. Internet users start to see the web as a utility that is expected to be operational on a permanent basis and to pose as little risk as water or electricity use.

F. Internet security problems can take multiple forms: spam, viruses, web squatting, fraud, copyright violation, denial of service, unauthorized entry into corporate or personal computers and networks (and theft or manipulation of the information stored in them), privacy infringements, fraud and harassment, among other possibilities. Some of these problems have acquired serious dimensions, and spam (unsolicited e-mail) is now proliferating at an alarming rate. By some estimates, in January 2003 about 25 percent of all e-mails that circulated on the Internet were unsolicited; by March the percentage was over 36 percent, and the 50 percent mark could be reached before the end of 2003. In 2001 the European Commission estimated that spam-related costs amounted to over 9.6 billion USD worldwide in connection charges alone. Other, more pessimistic estimates put the overall cost of spam to enterprises worldwide in 2003 at USD 20.5 billion. In addition to spammers operating for financial or other profit, often from offshore ISPs, spam is often used to carry out denial of service attacks. A number of techniques are available to combat spam, although spammers are also becoming increasingly sophisticated. In a growing number of countries, governments are considering or implementing anti-spam legislation.

G. Security incidents are not exclusively a problem of developed countries. Several developing countries rank among the countries that were targeted most often in digital attacks in 2002. However, attacks against government sites are less frequent than those against commercial entities, are driven by political factors, and have few economic consequences. Their most important effect may be that the media attention they attract helps undermine public confidence in the Internet in those countries where awareness of and trust in the Internet seem to be less advanced.

H. Most digital attacks in 2002 originated in a few countries, and 10 of them accounted for 80 percent of all attacks detected. The United States was at the top of the list. Security applications are commonly quoted as one of the areas where CEOs expect major developments in the medium term, and the IT security market is expanding fast. Total sales of IT security software, hardware and services are expected to reach USD 45 billion by 2006. The development of corporate initiatives in areas such as web services provides a strong incentive for IT security investment. Reasonable protection against Internet-generated risks can be achieved through a combination of software, hardware and risk management strategies that contemplate all potential sources of liability arising from interactions with customers, workers, suppliers and the general public. Studies based on reported security incidents assess internal threats as being as severe as external ones. In the end, the question of IT security at the firm level is much more a managerial problem than a technical one. It has to do with how penetrable the enterprise wants its business processes to be and how the risk management is integrated into those processes. While technology can help reduce those risks and costs, the key to a secure and private online environment is the combination of market efficiency and industry initiatives, political will and an appropriate legal environment.

The Development of Web Services

I. The concept of web services refers to automated interaction over the Internet between computers managing different business processes, in such a way that they generate a "grid" of computers in which each machine is able to feed other machines the input they require or obtain from them the information it needs. This interaction occurs via software that is designed to use other software. web services have the potential to significantly improve the efficiency of processes such as inventory control and routine purchasing. In the longer term, their use should extend to other business processes, as they enable seamless, automatic interoperability between the software applications used in running the various aspects of a business as well as with the applications of customers and suppliers.

J. Beyond that, web services will be an essential part of an economy in which "communication" between Internet-enabled objects will be increasingly important. Although the main impact of web services will be in enterprise operations, there are also many possibilities for consumer-oriented applications. For example, web services could be used to create virtual travel agents that give access to the reservation systems of airlines and railways, car rental companies and hotels, travel-related content providers, and so on.

K. The potential of web services to become an important factor of change derives from the fact that they lie at the junction of several strong currents. Some of these currents are changing business organization and interaction, and others could influence the future of computing. The first trend in business organization that influences the development of web services is the integration of supply chains and the move towards demand chain management. Another factor in the development of web services is the refocusing of enterprises, particularly larger ones, on those activities and processes that constitute the core of their business, and where their competitive advantage rests. The technology current moving web services forward is the mounting popularity of distributed computing, an approach in which computing resources are not concentrated in any particular place but pooled together in the network and used when and as needed, thus allowing more efficient allocation of resources.

Words and Expressions

comprehensive [ˌkɒmprɪˈhensɪv]	adj.	全面的
broadband [ˈbrɔːdbænd]	n.	宽带
subscription [səbˈskrɪpʃn]	n.	会员费，征订费
adopter [əˈdɒptə]	n.	采纳者；接收器
facility [fəˈsɪləti]	n.	附加服务，设施
envision [ɪnˈvɪʒn]	vt.	设想
spam [spæm]	n.	群发的垃圾邮件
infringement [ɪnˈfrɪndʒmənt]	n.	违反，对他人自由的侵犯
penetrable [ˈpenətrəbl]	adj.	可被穿透的，能穿透的
inventory [ˈɪnvəntɔːri]	n.	存货，清单

Unit 15 Some Technology Trends Affecting E-Business

Questions

***Directions:** In this section, you are required to answer the following questions according to the information in the text.*

(1) What is the main reason for subscribers to switch to broadband technologies?

(2) Why is someone willing to take the risk which every commercial transaction involves?

(3) Is web a utility that is safe like water or electricity use?

(4) How do you explain web services?

(5) What is the first factor in business organization that influences the development of web services?

Exercises

***Directions:** In this section, you are going to read ten statements attached to the text. Each statement contains information given in one of the paragraphs in the text. Identify, the paragraph from which the information is derived. You may choose a paragraph more than once.*

(1) Many new broadband subscribers have never accessed an Internet before.

(2) Some aspects of technology use have been particularly prominent in the e-business field and they will influence the development of e-business.

(3) The connection with several strong currents makes web services an important factor of change.

(4) A safe environment is no longer important for e-business than it is for business in the physical world.

(5) Although a number of initiatives aim at building new business models around broadband, no application has come into being with an influence on the functioning of markets or on the management of companies.

(6) Total sales of IT security software, hardware and services will probably reach 45 billion USD by 2006.

(7) Both developed and developing countries are involved in security incidents.

(8) Spam, viruses, web squatting, fraud, privacy infringements and some other possibilities are multiple forms of Internet security problems.

(9) Chances are that web services will greatly improve the efficiency of processes.

(10) Digital subscriber line and cable, which make dominant technologies, have an almost equal share of the world broadband market.

Translation

一些影响电子商务的技术趋势

下文将讨论在电子商务竞技场特别突出的一些技术应用,目的并不是详尽或全面地报道技术应用的各个方面,但这些技术应用可能会在今后几年对电子商务的发展产生影响。

宽带的发展

宽带互联网接入及其相关技术的传播是互联网流量快速增长的原因之一。宽带的传播不仅使得现有的互联网用户更加容易地交换信息,而且也吸引了新用户。一些运营商报告指出,30%～50%的新宽带用户以前从未购买过互联网订阅服务。

宽带的可利用性在过去的两年中发展很快,两项主要技术占有世界宽带市场几乎相同的份额:数字用户线路(DSL)宽带占50%,电缆宽带占45%。宽带的广泛采用是怎样影响商业活动的呢?快速的互联网接入是用户转向宽带技术的一个主要原因。因为数据流动更快,用户等待网页下载的时间更少,并且一直处在连接状态,所以宽带使用者乐于花费更多的时间来上网。与此同时,消费者将能够寻找到更多的信息,比较更多的选择,或者体验数字化产品。

关于宽带对企业组织或者企业之间的交易产生的影响,尽管很多初创者瞄准围绕宽带建立新的商务模式,但是还没有出现一种能够影响市场运作或公司管理的应用(与早期的互联网商业应用效果显著不同)。这并不是说宽带将不会对企业产生影响。事实上,企业比消费者购买了更多的在线内容,宽带使得这些内容更加容易获得,更容易使用,因而更适于销售,尤其是中小企业。宽带允许多个用户同时共享互联网连接,这样必然会降低单个用户的连接成本,这点同时也是中小企业考虑的一个重要因素。对于较大型的企业来说,将数据和应用集中于一个存储设备,而且让很多远程用户接入并能使用相当大数量的信息,可能会促进一些新的组织形式的采用。另外,宽带对于经济的更广泛的影响是可以预见的。除了改善对信息社会服务(如电子健康、电子教育、电子政务)的访问,这些间接但实实在在地对经济生产力产生了影响,和任何重大新技术一样,宽带的使用能够鼓励创新和刺激经济增长。

Unit 15 Some Technology Trends Affecting E-Business

安 全 问 题

一个安全的环境对电子商务来说和在现实世界里开展业务一样重要，每一笔商业交易都涉及一种风险，参与者通常对这些风险足够熟悉，足以判断预期的回报是否值得接受潜在损失的可能性。即使面临着巨大的风险，如果预期回报足够高，那么有人将会愿意承这个风险。当电子商务成为大部分人的日常生活的一部分，而且这些人比早期网络技术的应用者更不愿承风险时，各方面的安全就会变得至关重要。互联网用户开始将网络视为一种公共事业，希望它可以在一个永久性的基础上运作，并且可以像水或电的使用那样，产生尽量小的风险。

互联网安全问题的呈现形式有很多种：垃圾邮件、病毒、网络入侵、欺诈、侵犯著作权、拒绝服务、未经授权进入公司或者个人计算机和网络（以及对存储的信息进行偷窃或者操纵）、侵犯个人隐私、欺诈和骚扰，还有一些其他的可能性。其中一些问题已经达到了严重的程度，并且垃圾邮件（未经请求的电子邮件）正在以惊人的速度激增。据估计，2003年1月，在互联网上流转的邮件中大约25%都是垃圾邮件；到2003年3月，该比例超过了36%；在2003年年底前，则可能达到50%。在2001年，欧盟委员会曾评估，在世界范围内，仅连接费用和与垃圾邮件相关的损失总计超过96亿美元。其他更悲观的估计显示，垃圾邮件给全球企业在2003年带来的全部损失达到了205亿美元。除了一些为了财务或其他利益的垃圾邮件发送者外，其他来自国外的互联网服务提供商（ISP）的垃圾邮件经常用来执行拒绝服务的攻击。尽管垃圾邮件正在变得越来越"先进"，但是仍然有很多技术可以用来抗击垃圾邮件。在越来越多的国家，政府正在考虑或者实施反垃圾邮件的立法工作。

安全事故并非发达国家所独有的问题，许多发展中国家也被列入了在2002年遭受数字攻击最多的国家名单之中。然而，出于政治目的而对政府网站进行攻击的频率远低于那些对商业实体的攻击，这样的攻击也不致造成大的经济后果。这类攻击最主要的影响可能是吸引媒体的注意，以削弱那些互联网意识和信念都比较薄弱的国家的公众对互联网的信心。

2002年大部分的数字攻击都源自少数国家，其中10个国家占检测到的攻击的80%。美国位居榜首。安全应用程序一般被认为是首席执行官（CEO）希望在中期阶段获得显著进步的一个领域，并且网络信息技术安全市场扩展很快。到2006年，网络信息技术安全软件、硬件和业务的总销售额预计可达450亿美元。公司在诸如网络服务等领域的发展将会给网络信息技术安全投资提供强大的动力。对互联网产生的风险进行合理的保护可以通过软件、硬件和风险管理等组合策略实现，而这种组合策略是通过对与来自用户、员工、供应商和公众的互动后所产生的所有潜在责任进行反复思考后得出的。基于已发生的安全事故来分析内部威胁，和分析外部威胁同等重要。最终，公司级别的网络信息技术安全与其说是一个技术问题，不如说是一个管理问题。这与企业希望它的业务流程具有怎样的渗透性，以及如何将风险管理融入这些过程中紧密相关。虽然技术可以帮助降低这些风险和成本，但创造一个安全和私有的在线环境的关键就是把市场效率和产业动力、政治意愿和一个适当的法律环境结合起来。

网络服务的发展

网络服务的概念是指通过互联网让管理不同业务流程的计算机实现自动化的交互，以这种方式产生一种计算机"网格"，在"网格"中，每个计算机既可以为其他计算机提供所需的输入，也可向其他计算机请求它自己所需的信息。这种交互通过能够调用其他软件的软件来实现。网络服务具有显著改善诸如存货控制和日常采购等流程效率的潜力。长远来看，它们的使用将进一步扩展到其他业务流程，因为它们可以实现各类运行业务的软件应用程序之间无缝隙、自动化的交互操作，也同样适用于客户和供应商之间的此类交互操作。

除此以外，网络服务也将成为经济的一个重要组成部分，在这一经济中，在可上网的对象之间实现"通信"将变得日益重要。尽管网络服务的主要影响是在企业运作层面上，但是对于很多以客户为导向的应用程序也可能有许多影响。比如，网络服务可以被用来建立虚拟旅游代理机构，以准许用户访问航空和铁路公司、汽车出租公司、宾馆以及与旅游相关的内容提供商等的预订系统。

网络服务成为变化的一个重要因素的潜力来自这样一个事实，即网络服务正处于几股强大潮流的交汇点。其中的一些趋势正在改变企业组织和交互性，还有其他的一些趋势将会影响计算的未来。在商业组织中，影响网络服务发展的第一个趋势是供应链集成和转向需求链管理。在网络服务发展的另一个因素是企业，重新聚焦于能形成它们业务核心的活动和流程，以及它们的竞争优势，特别是大型企业。推动网络服务向前发展的技术趋势是日益普及的分布式计算，这种方法并不是把计算资源集中在任何特定的区域，而是在任何需要使用的时候，通过网络将计算资源聚集在一起，从而更有效地分配资源。

UNIT 16　E-Business Relies on Security

A. E-bsiness security is evolving from the old notion of turning the enterprise into an information fortress to a new, more comprehensive model of privacy and trusted e-business.

B. The old view of security involved keeping the "bad guys" out by using firewalls, virus protection, and intrusion detection software.

C. The new view adds the model of trusted e-business: letting the "good guys" in. These good guys are customers, partners, remote employees, or others upon whom your e-business depends. Giving them access is the very basis of e-business, but allowing partners, customers, and sometimes even competitors inside the e-business infrastructure adds levels of complexity far beyond the traditional model of security. Customer trust depends upon keeping personal information private and secure.

D. Creating a high-performance e-business security infrastructure demands close coordination of both technical and management policies and procedures. The time and costs associated with monitoring all external connections, internal activities, and vulnerabilities are overwhelming Information Technology Supporting (IS) departments and corporate executives alike. As a result, many corporations must rethink the overall network strategy and its effectiveness in enabling enterprise-wide business objectives.

E. When implementing a new security solution, an enterprise must have many goals in mind. These include:

(1) Mitigating and managing security risks. This is the traditional role of security—keeping intruders out and keeping information safe and must be maintained.

(2) Privacy—protecting personal and corporate information. This is one of the biggest changes in the security market: greater demand to share information with customers and partners

is putting new stress on companies to prevent that information from falling into the wrong hands. Data control and management is a critical issue for corporations. Customer information is a valuable asset and must be protected.

(3) Quickly deploying secure e-business initiatives. Security solutions must keep time-to-market issues in mind, allowing the e-business environment to be modified on the fly without compromising security.

(4) Reducing ongoing costs of managing and administering security. Return on Investment (ROI) is always a key goal, and many companies consider outsourcing security administration because they can use the latest solutions without buying new products or hiring new expertise.

Security Requirements for E-business

F. The security infrastructure needs to have the following basic capabilities:

(1) Identification / authentication. This is the first step of any security and privacy process: being able to tell who users are. Having a security infrastructure that can do this quickly and accurately is necessary for creating a good experience for customers and partners.

(2) Authorization. Once the system determines who users are—and that they are who they say they are—it must provide the correct levels of access to different applications and stores of information.

(3) Asset protection. The system must keep information confidential and private. This has become more difficult in the modern e-business environment, where information is traveling across multiple, often untrusted, networks.

(4) Accountability. This is the ability to keep track of who has done what with what data. E-business solutions also need to ensure that participants in transactions are accountable.

(5) Administration. This involves defining security policies and implementing them consistently across the enterprise infrastructure's different platforms and networks.

(6) Assurance. This demands mechanisms that show the security solutions are working, through methods such as proactive detection of viruses or intrusions, periodic reports, incident recording, and so forth.

(7) Availability. Modern e-businesses must prevent interruptions of service, even during major attacks. This means that the solution must have built-in fault tolerance and applications and procedures to quickly bring systems back online. IT managers must be able to make changes to the system 7×24.

Privacy for E-business

G. The whole issue of security in an e-business environment has evolved to encompass issues of privacy and trust.

H. Security does not always entail privacy, but privacy requires security. Keeping information confidential requires much more than a technology solution. It is about business policy and the processes they support.

I. Data privacy is about choice: the freedom of individuals to choose how they wish to be treated by organizations that control data that describes them. Data privacy has emerged as a major societal issue as individuals have begun to question the levels of technological intrusiveness they will tolerate.

J. Privacy includes several aspects. First and foremost, privacy enables companies to protect personal and organizational assets, such as information about customers and partners; these "good guys" must be let in to access and modify this data, without unauthorized users being able to see it.

Infrastructure and Policy

K. Security and privacy must be built directly into the infrastructure. Privacy is a matter of policy: determining who can see what within the corporate IT environment. But any privacy policy is only as good as the security infrastructure that backs it up. The security infrastructure is vital to the ongoing relationship with partners and customers.

L. The combination of security infrastructure and a sound privacy policy creates an environment of trust among partners and other users. This protects not only users but also enterprises that hold that data—and which could be held liable for its loss.

M. Businesses can harness their customer's desire for privacy controls into a strategic competitive advantage. On the other hand, a company needs to be aware of the impact of losing control of customer information.

Implementation of E-business Security

N. Installing an e-business security solution includes creating a blueprint of security needs, selecting skills and resources, and implementation.

O. Enterprises should recognize the need to implement security and privacy solutions that can span the "end-to-end" e-business environment. These systems must provide a range of security controls, including intrusion detection, authentication and authorization tools, vulnerability scanning, incident management, and firewall administration. The system must take into account data control processes for sensitive information.

P. This infrastructure must support a comprehensive common security and privacy model that can expand to new applications and resources. This enables companies to lower their total cost of ownership (TCO), focus on their core competencies, and rest assured their networks are maintained with the latest technologies applicable to their particular needs and vertical industry.

Planning: The Blueprint

Q. The first step in the process is creating a blueprint by assessing security needs and determining how to address them. By definition, these needs should align with the company's business objectives. There are several stages in creating this blueprint. The assessment stage establishes a baseline or initial diagnosis of the overall security posture. Within the assessment stage are two main pillars: the technical and the business components.

R. Technical assessments generally involve two main aspects: a vulnerability assessment to determine system weaknesses and a threat assessment to determine likely threats. The business assessment can contain the following aspects:

(1) Physical environment assessment covers the actual office and hardware.

(2) Incident response assessment reviews the processes necessary to restore functionality in the event of attack or other incident.

(3) Information protection assessment examines all policies, procedures, and controls with respect to information access and retention.

(4) A privacy health check will evaluate all of the current processes and procedures, as well as levels of adherence. This check will also evaluate risk of disclosure of confidential data.

(5) Security awareness assessment of employees.

S. The next step in the blueprint process is an architectural analysis, which is designed to look at the security solutions already in place and determine what aspects must change. Then the company must create a security strategy plan to implement these changes.

Selection Process for Skills and Resources

T. Once the security and privacy needs have been outlined, a company needs to determine if it has the necessary skills in-house to implement the blueprint. Some companies will have all the necessary skills in-house, while others must outsource some or all of the implementation.

U. When looking at possible vendors, which come from many backgrounds, companies must ask and receive answers to the following types of questions:

(1) Does the service provider have the necessary experience (backed by customer examples and reference accounts) to overcome the security challenges associated with a particular vertical industry or individual business?

(2) Have the necessary capital investments been made in tools, staffing, global infrastructure, and support?

(3) Does the service provider have alliances with other key industry players to deliver an integrated security service, or is it operating in a vacuum? Are these just "paper alliances", or are they well-coordinated and market tested? If outsourcing with multiple vendors, which vendor would act as the "prime", and would one have contact with the other solutions vendors?

(4) Is the provider able to not only implement security solutions but also manage them on an ongoing basis if needed?

(5) Does the provider take into account privacy issues for empowering customers to control their own information? Examples of privacy issues include opt-in or opt-out controls for information gathering, data handling procedures, and data retention standards.

Implementation

V. Once these questions have been answered, the enterprise enters the implementation stage. On the technical side, a combination of the assessment, architecture analysis, and strategy and planning stages will determine whether the hardware and software requirements are fulfilled.

W. Consequently, integration best practices involve the creation of a pilot implementation, which can be performance-tested and debugged before migration to the new solution. This practice is designed to limit downtime, complications, or disruption in business service. Testing and debug services will also continue to play a key role in the implementation of information security engagements because the testing data from such services is used to calculate network device management thresholds and performance baselines.

X. Several human factors should also be considered, such as training, staffing, and processes. A perfectly executed integration of the security system is rendered helpless if the IT staff has no idea how to operate, manage, and maintain the network.

Y. Precisely documented policies, procedures, and specifications, in addition to education and training of IT personnel, are critical success factors.

Conclusion

Z. As security and privacy threats grow in both scope and sophistication, forward-thinking organizations of all shapes and sizes will continue to strengthen their defenses against these threats.

I. Some organizations will continue to rely on internal systems and resources to manage the "cyber risks" associated with operating in the new economy. Others, however, may lack the training, skills, resources, or interest needed to operate their IT infrastructure securely and will subsequently turn to outside experts for help.

II. Whether a company looks outside or in-house to implement a new security infrastructure, it must take a series of specific steps. Without following this blueprint, a company cannot hope to create a system that is both secure and up to date, encompassing the divergent needs of greater information sharing and greater privacy.

Words and Expressions

overwhelming [ˌəʊvəˈwelmɪŋ]	adj.	压倒性的，强悍而令人难以应对的
deploy [dɪˈplɔɪ]	v.	部署
proactive [ˌprəʊˈæktɪv]	adj.	积极行动的
entail [ɪnˈteɪl]	v.	牵连，导致
vulnerability [ˌvʌlnərəˈbɪlətɪ]	n.	脆弱
baseline [ˈbeɪslaɪn]	n.	基础，起点
retention [rɪˈtenʃn]	n.	保留
debug [ˌdiːˈbʌg]	v.	〈计算机程序〉纠错
sophistication [səˌfɪstɪˈkeɪʃn]	n.	老练，复杂性
divergent [daɪˈvɜːdʒənt]	adj.	不同的，有分歧的

Questions

(1) What is the difference between the old and new notion of e-business security?

(2) What goal must an enterprise have in mind when implementing a new security solution?

(3) What is the relationship between privacy and security?

(4) What is the privacy and what is the most important aspect of it?

(5) What should we pay attention to in implementing security and privacy solutions?

Exercises

Directions: In this section, you are required to answer the questions with T or F.

T (for True) if the statement agrees with the information given in the passage;

F (for False) if the statement contradicts the information given in the passage.

(1) E-business security is developing from the old notion of changing the enterprise into an information fortress to a new, more comprehensive model of e-business.

(2) Implementing a new security solution, an enterprise has only one important goal, that is to protect personal and corporate information.

(3) Security solutions must keep time-to-market issues in mind.

(4) Once the system determines who users are, it must provide the correct levels of access to the same applications and stores of information.

(5) The security issue in an e-business environment has evolved to encompass issues of privacy and trust.

(6) Security enables companies to protect personal and organizational assets.

(7) Security and privacy must be built indirectly into the infrastructure.

(8) The infrastructure must support a comprehensive common security and privacy model.

(9) Creating a blueprint by assessing security needs and determining how to address them.

(10) Once the security and privacy needs have been outlined, a company does not need to determine if it has the necessary skills in-house to implement the blueprint.

Translation

电子商务依赖于安全性

电子商务安全正在从"把企业转变成一个信息堡垒"的旧观念向新的、更全面的隐私和可信电子商务模式演进。

旧的安全观包括使用防火墙、病毒保护以及入侵检测软件将"不怀好意的人"挡在外面。

新的观点引入了电子商务的信任模式:让"好人"进来。这里的"好人"指的是客户、合作伙伴、远程雇员或者其他任何电子商务所依赖的个体。让"好人"能够访问系统是电子商务最基本的条件,但是允许合作伙伴、客户,甚至你的竞争对手进入电子商务系统,带来的复杂性将会远远超出传统安全模式。客户信任建立在个人隐私保护和安全上。

构建一个高绩效的电子商务安全基础框架(或体系),需要技术与管理制度和程序的紧密配合。与监控所有的外部链接、内部活动和漏洞相关的时间和成本使信息技术支持部门和企业高管不堪重负。因此,许多公司必须重新考虑整体网络战略及其在实现企业范围业务目标方面的有效性。

在实施一个新的安全解决方案时,一个企业必须牢记多个方面的目标。这些目标包括:

(1)减轻和管理安全风险。这是安全的传统角色——拒入侵者于门外,同时保证信息的安全性,并且必须长期坚持。

(2)隐私——保护个人和企业信息。这是安全市场的重大变化之一:与客户和合作伙伴共享信息的需求更大,在如何防止这些信息被恶意利用方面,给公司带来了新的压力。对公司而言,数据控制和管理是一个关键问题。客户信息是一份很有价值的资产,必须得到保护。

(3)快速部署安全电子商务行动。安全解决方案必须牢记"时间即市场"的思想,应允许电子商务环境在不影响安全性的前提下对系统进行动态修改。

(4)降低管理和安全管理的持续成本。投资回报率(ROI)一直都是一个关键的目标,许多公司考虑将安全管理的职能外包,因为这样可以及时采用最新的安全措施,而不必去购买新设备或者雇佣新的专家。

电子商务的安全需求

安全基础设施需要具备以下基本功能:

(1)身份认证/实名认证。这是实施任何安全和隐私方法的第一步,目的是识别出用户身份。一个能够快速而准确地进行身份/实名认证的安全基础设施对于给客户和合作伙伴创造一个愉快体验而言是必需的。

(2)授权。一旦系统识别出用户的身份——也就是说他们确实与其所表明的身份相一致,那么系统就应该向其提供相应级别的进入不同的应用和信息存储的权限。

(3)资产保护。系统必须保持信息的机密性和隐私性。这对现代电子商务环境而言是比较困难的,因为在电子商务环境中,信息是通过多重的,有时甚至是不可信任的网络环境传播的。

(4)责任性。这是一种跟踪用户对数据所做的处理记录的能力。电子商务解决方案也需要确保交易的参与者是能够承担责任的。

(5)执行。这涉及明确安全策略,以及在企业基础架构的不同平台和网络中统一实施这些策略。

(6)保证。这要求有一个能够显示安全解决方案有效的机制,如主动检测病毒或者入侵的、定期报告、事件记录等。

(7)有效性。现代的电子商务系统必须能够防止服务中断的发生,哪怕是在受到重大攻击时也要如此。这就是说,解决方案必须要有内置的容错机制,以及在线快速恢复的应用和程序。网络信息技术经理必须能够对系统进行 7×24 的调整。

电子商务的私密性

电子商务环境的整个安全问题已经发展到了关乎隐私和信任问题的阶段。

安全性并不总是牵涉隐私,但是隐私性却要求得到安全保证。保持信息的私密性所需的不仅仅是一个技术解决方案,它涉及业务的政策以及它们所支持的流程。

数据隐私实际上是一个选择问题:每个个体都自由选择如何被那些掌握有关他们的信息的机构对待。由于个体开始质疑他们要承受多大程度上的技术入侵,所以数据私密性已经成为一个主要的社会问题。

隐私包括几个方面:首先,隐私确保企业能够保护个人和组织的财产,比如客户和合作伙伴的信息;这些"好人"应被允许进入访问并能修改相关数据信息,同时保证未被授权的使用者看不到这些数据。

基础设施与政策

安全和隐私必须直接建立到基础设施中。隐私是一个政策问题：明确企业在网络信息技术环境下能看到什么内容。但是，任何隐私政策最多只能达到安全基础设施所支持的安全程度。安全基础设施对于维护现有的客户和合作伙伴的关系是至关重要的。

安全基础设施与完善隐私政策的结合，在商业伙伴和其他用户之间创造了一个相互信任的环境。这样的方式不仅保护了用户，同时也保护了拥有那些数据的企业，并且可以让企业对数据的丢失承担责任。

一方面，企业可以把满足客户对隐私控制的需求转变为一种战略上的竞争优势；另一方面，企业也必须意识到失去对客户信息的控制所产生的影响。

电子商务安全的实施

建立一个电子商务安全解决方案包括：规划安全需求的蓝图，选择相应的技能和资源并组织实施。

企业应该认识到这样一种需求，即实现跨越"端到端"电子商务环境的安全和隐私解决方案的需求。这些系统必须提供一系列的安全控制，包括入侵检测、认证和授权工具、漏洞扫描、突发事件处理和防火墙监控。系统还必须考虑敏感信息的数据控制流程。

这种基础设施必须支持全面的通用安全和隐私模型，以便扩展到新的应用程序和资源。这样可使企业降低总拥有成本（TCO），关注核心竞争力，并确保它们的网络是采用最新的技术维护的，可用来满足特定需求和适应垂直行业需求。

计划：蓝图

这一过程的第一步是评估安全需求并确定如何满足这些需求，并以此制订出蓝图。根据定义，这些需求应该与企业的商业目标一致。制订蓝图有几个阶段：在评估阶段，创建一个全面的关于安全状况的基准或初步的诊断。在评估阶段主要有两个支柱：技术部分和业务部分。

技术评估通常涉及两个主要方面：确定系统弱点的漏洞评估和决定可能威胁的威胁评估。业务评估则包括以下几个方面：

（1）物理环境评估，评估覆盖实际办公设施和硬件设施；

（2）事件响应评估，检测在遇到攻击事件或其他不测时系统恢复功能所需的必要流程；

（3）信息保护评估，检查所有的政策、程序以及有关信息访问和保存的控制；

（4）隐私健康检查，评估当前所有的处理流程和程序，以及执行的程度，这一检查也将评估泄露机密数据的风险；

（5）雇员的安全意识评估。

制订蓝图的第二个步骤是架构分析。它旨在检查已经实施了的安全解决方案，并且确定哪些方面还需要改进。之后，企业就必须制订安全策略计划去实施这些改进方案。

技能和资源的选择过程

一旦大致勾勒出了安全和私密需求，公司就要确定其是否有足够的技术能力来实现这个蓝图。一些公司将在内部拥有所有必需的技术能力，与此同时，另外一些公司必须外包部分或者全部的实施工作。

在考虑具有不同背景的潜在供应商时，公司必须提出以下各类问题并得到相应的答案：

（1）服务供应商是否具有必要的经验（由客户案例和参考账户支持）来克服与特定的垂直行业或单个企业相关的安全性挑战？

（2）在工具、人员、全球基础设施和支持方面是否具有足够的资金投入？

（3）服务供应商是否和其他关键行业主导者联盟，提供集成化的信息安全服务，或者还是处在隔绝状态中独自运作？这些仅仅是"纸上谈兵式的联盟"，还是已经合作良好并得到了市场的检验？如果把业务外包给多个供应商，那么哪个供应商能够扮演"主角"？一个供应商是否能和其他解决方案供应商保持联系？

（4）服务供应商是否不仅能够实施安全解决方案，而且还能够在需要的时候进行持续管理？

（5）服务供应商是否考虑过授权给客户来控制他们信息的隐私？隐私问题的例子包括信息收集的流入与流出控制、数据处理程序和数据存储标准。

实　施

一旦这些问题得到解决，企业便进入实施阶段。从技术角度讲，评估、结构分析、策略及计划阶段的结合将决定硬件和软件需求是否得以满足。

因此，集成的最优实践牵涉创建一个实施试点，在迁移到新的解决方案之前先对它进行性能测试和调试。这一做法旨在减少停工时间、降低复杂性或预防商业服务的中断。测试和调试服务将继续在信息安全项目中扮演重要角色，因为来自这些服务的测试数据用于计算网络设备的管理阈值和性能基线。

许多人为因素也应该被考虑，如培训、人员配置和流程。如果网络信息技术人员不知道如何运行、管理和维护网络，那么无论多完美的安全系统实施集成都是徒劳无益的。

除了对网络信息技术人员的教育和培训之外，详细准确的文档化的政策、程序和说明文件都是成功的关键因素。

结　论

随着安全和隐私的威胁在范围和复杂程度上的不断增加，各种类型和规模的有前瞻意识的组织将会继续强化它们对这些威胁的防御能力。

一些机构将继续依赖内部系统和资源来监控其在新经济下运营的相关的"网络风险"。但是，其他的一些机构可能缺乏安全运作他们的网络信息技术基础设施所需要的培训、技能、资源或兴趣，最终只能向外部专家寻求帮助。

一个公司不管是通过外部还是内部实行一种新的安全基础架构，都必须采取一系列特定的步骤。如果不依照这一蓝图，一个企业就不能建立起这样一个既安全又现代化的，同时还能满足更加多样化的信息共享和更高级别隐私需求的系统。

UNIT 17: UNCTAD B2C E-Commerce Index 2017

Introduction

A. This report presents the 2017 edition of The UNCTAD Business-to-Consumer (B2C) E-Commerce Index (Index), which was first introduced in the Information Economy Report 2015: Unlocking the Potential of E-Commerce for Developing Countries (UNCTAD, 2015) and updated in April 2016 (UNCTAD, 2016). The indicators used in the Index are explained, a new payment indicator is introduced and the Index is updated with the latest available data.

Components of the Index

B. The Index reflects the processes involved in an online shopping B2C transaction. Some type of web presence is required by the seller to accept online orders. The process also requires Internet access on the part of users to place an order. A payment method is needed on delivery. Finally, the product must be delivered to the customer's home or at a pick-up point.

Internet users

C. The starting point is that consumers need Internet access to order a product online.

B2C web presence

D. The availability of secure Internet servers is included in the Index as a proxy for the readiness of a country to enable secure transactions online. Secure servers use encryption technology in online transactions to protect the transfer of data from unauthorized interception.

Delivery

E. Any physical good ordered online must be delivered. In the original B2C E-Commerce Index, the indicator selected was the proportion of the population that received postal delivery at home. Following consultation with the Universal Postal Union (UPU), another indicator was chosen for the 2016 Index: the UPU postal reliability score (UNCTAD, 2016).

Payment

F. Products ordered over the Internet can be paid for online or offline. Products purchased from online shops can be paid for in different ways. Payment methods vary among countries and are a function of national financial regulations, credit riskiness, vendor strategies and consumer preferences. This makes it difficult to choose a single payment method for measuring e-commerce payment readiness. Credit and debit cards are the most popular payment method worldwide in terms of online transaction purchase value. Therefore, credit card penetration among the population aged 15 years and older, collected as part of the World Bank's Global Findex survey, was used as the payment indicator for the Index in previous editions. A new payment indicator is introduced for the 2017 Index.

G. Having an account (including mobile money) shows a higher correlation with online shopping (R^2=0.68) than the credit card indicator that has so far been included in the Index (R^2=0.58) (see Fig. 17.1). This is a strong reason for replacing the old indicator with the use of accounts.

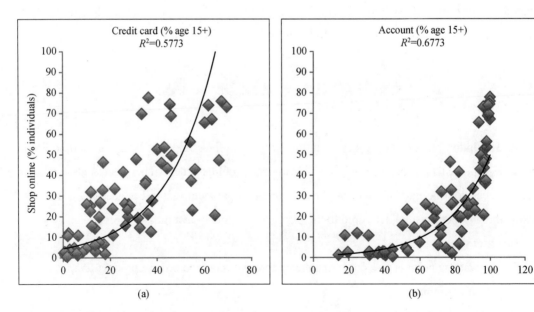

Fig. 17.1 Credit Card and Account Compared with Shopping Online (% of Individuals), 2014
Source: Adapted from FINDEX and UNCTAD.

H. The introduction of this new indicator affects the Index rankings (see Fig. 17.2). The share of the population aged 15 and above with an account benefits countries with relatively limited use of credit cards but high incidence of bank and mobile money accounts. As a result, Kenya, which has a high penetration of mobile money, climbs 13 positions in the Index. Another example is the Netherlands, which has relatively low credit card penetration compared to other developed economies. However, virtually all people aged 15 and above (99 percent) have a bank account in that country.

I. Any indicator that is a proxy for online payment affects the Index for economies where there is a high incidence of cash used to pay for e-commerce purchases (cash on delivery accounted for 7 percent of global payments in 2015). For example, in Egypt, around 90 percent of e-commerce transactions are paid by cash-on-delivery, and in LDCs, the reliance on cash is even more pronounced (UNCTAD, 2017).

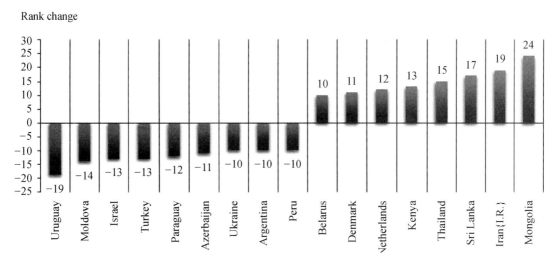

Fig. 17.2 Impact of New Payment Indicator

Note: Economies with a ± 10 change.

Source: Adapted from UNCTAD.

Data Sources and Country Coverage

J. Until 2016, the index was calculated using a different payment indicator. Using the 2017 methodology for the Index, the scores for previous years have also been calculated to better illustrate change. The coverage has improved to 144 economies, up by seven from the 2016 edition. The changes introduced in the Index are summarized in Table 17.1.

Table 17.1   Changes in the UNCTAD B2C E-Commerce Index

2014 B2C E-Commerce Index	2016 B2C E-Commerce Index	2017 B2C E-Commerce Index
4 indicators: • Internet users • Secure servers • Credit card penetration • Postal delivery at home	4 indicators: • Internet users • Secure servers • Credit card penetration • Postal reliability score	4 indicators: • Internet users • Secure servers • Account penetration • Postal reliability score
130 economies	137 economies	144 economies

K. The Index can be used to estimate the proportion of population shopping online. This is compared with official published statistics. As a result of the changes made, the 2017 edition shows a higher degree of correlation with the share of the population shopping online (see Fig. 17.3). The R^2 value rose from 0.73 in 2016 to 0.79 in 2017.

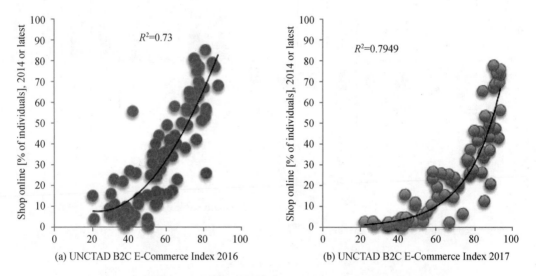

(a) UNCTAD B2C E-Commerce Index 2016   (b) UNCTAD B2C E-Commerce Index 2017

Fig. 17.3   Correlation Between UNCTAD B2C E-Commerce Index 2016 and 2017 and the Share of Individuals Shopping Online

Source: UNCTAD.

Results

L. The top ten economies in the UNCTAD B2C E-commerce Index 2017 are shown in Table 17.2. Luxembourg remains the top performer. Six of the top ten economies are also in the top ten of economies with the highest proportion of Internet shoppers. This suggests a generally high explanatory association between the variables contained in the Index and online shopping. Among the top ten, the Republic of Korea and Japan stand out by having a lower actual proportion of online shoppers than predicted by the Index value. This may reflect factors not contained in the Index, such as a preference for shopping in physical stores, lack of trust and other factors (UNCTAD, 2016 and Ipsos, 2017). Notable improvements include Switzerland, which rose from 8th to 2nd, the United Kingdom, which rose from 10th to 6th and Germany, which rose from 14th to 9th. These gains are all largely due to a rise in postal reliability. It should be noted that the top 10 economies are tightly clustered with the difference between first and tenth separated by only four value points.

Table 17.2   Top 10 Economies in the UNCTAD B2C E-Commerce Index 2017

2017 Rank	Economy	Share of individuals using Internet (2016)	Share of individuals with an account (15+, 2014 or latest)	Secure Internet servers per 1 million people (normalized, 2016)	UPU postal	Index Value (2016 data)	Index Value (2015 data)	Index Rank
1	Luxembourg	97	96	98	94	96.5	97	1
2	Switzerland	89	98	100	99	96.4	94	8
3	Norway	97	100	96	93	96.4	95	3
4	Netherlands	90	99	99	95	95.9	96	2
5	Republic of Korea	93	94	96	99	95.5	95	4
6	United Kingdom	95	99	92	95	95.1	93	10
7	Sweden	92	100	94	93	94.6	95	7
8	Japan	92	97	89	97	93.8	94	9
9	Germany	90	99	93	92	93.5	92	14
10	New Zealand	88	100	90	95	93.3	93	11

Source: UNCTAD.

M. Table 17.3 shows the average values by geographic region. There are wide regional differences. In the case of Internet access, less than a quarter of the population in Africa uses the Internet compared to two thirds in Western Asia. The relative strengths and weaknesses generally differ. East, South and Southeast Asia needs to boost Internet penetration, which currently stands at below half of the population on average, as well as the number of secure servers, which are also below world average. In Latin America and the Caribbean, Internet penetration is average as are secure servers and the main barriers would appear to be relatively poor postal reliability and relatively few people with financial accounts. To facilitate more inclusive e-commerce, African countries would seek to catch up in all policy areas.

Table 17.3 Regional Values for the UNCTAD B2C E-Commerce Index, 2017

Region	Share of individuals using Internet (2016)	Secure Internet servers per 1 million people (normalized, 2016)	UPU postal reliability score (2016)	Share of individuals with an account (15+, 2014 or latest)	UNCTAD B2C e-commerce Index value
Africa	23	31	31	29	28
East, South and Southeast Asia	46	51	63	58	54
Latin America and the Caribbeans	51	57	34	46	47
Western Asia	67	59	50	56	58
Transition economies	64	59	66	49	59
Developed Countries	83	88	86	92	87
World	52	56	54	55	54

N. According to UPU, the volatility in the Postal Reliability Score has several possible explanations:

(1) An improved capture of tracking events and data (the trend is usually to a higher quality of tracking data capture over time);

(2) The introduction of revised postal processes in a number of countries following the huge growth of e-commerce related items;

(3) A number of postal networks could have confronted bottlenecks related to this surge in e-commerce volumes;

(4) The composition of e-commerce flows and postal flows might have changed in a number of countries (for instance transporting and delivering heavier goods and more expensive goods resulting in more delivery delays) so the results might be dependent on the kind of product or service being delivered to the final customer.

Conclusions

O. There are ongoing efforts to improve the Index and to make it as relevant as possible. In 2016, the UPU Reliability Index score was introduced. In 2017, the availability of a bank or mobile money account replaced credit card penetration. The 2017 edition has a higher predictive capability of online shopping than the previous indexes (see Fig. 17.4). Changes in the composition of an Index always imply a break in the time series. However, two years of results were calculated for the 2017 Index, the beginning of a time series that over time will allow countries to better gauge their progress in the enablers of B2C e-commerce.

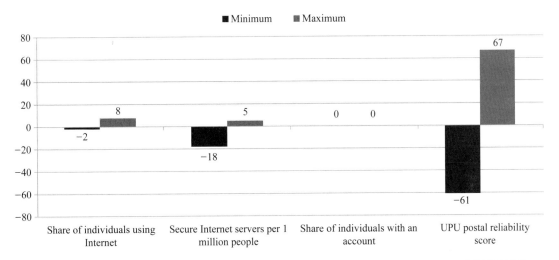

Fig. 17.4 Minimum and Maximum Changes in Value, by Indicator Included in the UNCTAD B2C E-Commerce Index, Using 2015 and 2016 Data

Source: UNCTAD.

P. Only some of the countries in the UNCTAD B2C E-Commerce Index have data on the actual share of the population in a country buying online. However, the available data show great variation between countries, ranging from as much as 80 percent in Denmark to less than 1 percent in Zimbabwe. In many developing and transition economies, online shoppers continue to represent a small proportion of the population, whereas in most developed economies more than half of the population are buying goods or services online.

Words and Expressions

indicator [ˈɪndɪkeɪtə]	n.	指示物
update [ˌʌpˈdeɪt]	v.	更新，给……提供最新消息
	n.	更新信息，快讯
proxy [ˈprɒksi]	n.	代表权
debit [ˈdebɪt]	n.	借方
	v.	记入借方账户
escrow [ˈeskrəʊ]	n.	暂交第三者保管的金钱（或资产）
transfer [trænsˈfɜː]	n.	转移，调动
	v.	转移，移交
virtually [ˈvɜːtʃuəli]	adv.	事实上
penetration [ˌpenɪˈtreɪʃn]	n.	进入，穿透
drawback [ˈdrɔːbæk]	n.	缺点，障碍
explanatory [ɪkˈsplænətri]	adj.	解释性的

Questions

Directions: In this section, you are required to answer the following questions according to the information in the text.

(1) Can you briefly describe the 2017 edition of the UNCTAD Business-to-Consumer (B2C) E-Commerce Index?

(2) What does the UNCTAD B2C E-Commerce Index reflect?

(3) What does the UNCTAD B2C E-Commerce Index consists of?

(4) What is implied in the fact that the Republic of Korea and Japan stand out among the top ten economies?

(5) According to UPU, how do we explain the volatility in the Postal Reliability Score?

Exercises

Directions: In this section, there are five questions and for each of them there are four choices marked A, B, C and D. You should decide on the best choice.

(1) Products purchased from online shops can be paid for _____.

    A. by credit card   B. in cash

    C. by debit card   D. in different ways

(2) Compared with the credit card indicator, having an account (including mobile money) shows a _____ correlation with online shopping.

   A. higher   B. same   C. lower   D. no

(3) In Egypt, around 90 percent of e-commerce transactions are paid by _____.

   A. credit card   B. cash-on-delivery

   C. Alipay   D. all of the above

(4) What can we learn about the top ten economies in the UNCTAD B2C E-Commerce Index 2017?

   A. Switzerland remained the top performer.

   B. Switzerland had notable improvements.

   C. The United Kingdom dropped its rank.

   D. Luxembourg ranked the top.

(5) Which of the following statements is TRUE?

   A. There are narrow region differences about the average values.

   B. Two thirds of population in Africa uses the Internet.

   C. East, South and Southeast Asia needs to boost Internet penetration.

   D. A large number of people have opened their financial accounts.

2017年联合国贸易和发展会议 B2C 电子商务指数

引　言

本报告介绍了2017年联合国贸易和发展会议B2C电子商务指数（下称"指数"），该指数首次出现在《2015年信息经济报告：为激发发展中国家电子商务的潜力》（联合国贸易和发展会议，2015年）中，并在2016年4月做了更新（联合国贸易和发展会议，2016年）。本报告对指数中使用的指标做了解释，引进了新的支付指标，并根据最新的数据更新了指数。

指数的组成部分

指数反映了在线购物B2C交易所涉及的过程。卖方接受在线订单需要使用特定类型的网站。该过程还要求客户在网上下订单。交货时需要选择付款方式。最后，产品必须送到客户的家中或拾取点。

互联网用户

消费者需要通过互联网访问才能在线订购产品。

B2C网站

指数中包含安全服务器，作为一个国家安全进行在线交易的代理。安全服务器使用加密技术来保护在线交易中的数据传输免受未经授权的拦截。

运输

在线订购的所有实物商品必须邮寄。在最初的指数中，选择的指标是在家中接收邮政投递的人口比例。在与万国邮政联盟（UPU）协商后，2016年指数选择了另一个指标：万国邮政联盟的可靠性得分（联合国贸易和发展会议，2016年）。

付款

通过互联网订购的产品可以在线或离线支付。通过在线商店购买的产品可以采用不同方式付款。付款方式因国家/地区而异，并且取决于国家/地区的金融法规、信用风险、供应商策略和消费者偏好。很难选择一种单一的支付方式来衡量电子商务的支付准备情况。就在线交易的购买价值而言，信用卡和借记卡是全球最受欢迎的支付方式。因此,世界银行在Findex调查中收集了15岁及以上人口的信用卡普及率,在早期版本的指数中用作支付指标。2017年指数引入了新的支付指标。

拥有账户(包括手机钱包)与在线购物的相关度(R^2=0.68),比信用卡指标与在线购物的相关度(R^2=0.58)更高(见图17.1),这就是用账户指标替换旧指标的有力支撑。

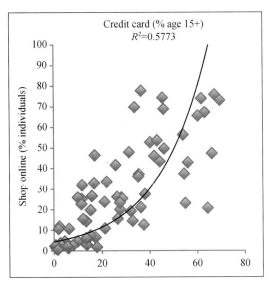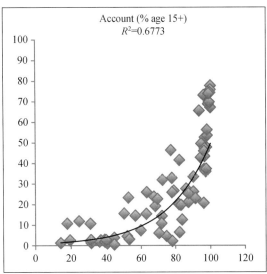

图17.1　信用卡和账户与在线购物比(个人百分比),2014

资料来源:FINDEX和UNCTAD。

这一新指标的引入会影响指数排名(见图17.2)。"15岁及以上拥有账户的人口比例"这一指标有利于信用卡使用相对有限,但银行和移动货币账户使用率较高的国家。因此,手机钱包普及率较高的肯尼亚在该指数排名中上升了13位。另一个例子是荷兰,与其他发达经济体相比,信用卡普及率相对较低。但是,几乎所有15岁及以上的人(99%)都在该国拥有银行账户。

在较多使用现金支付电子商务购买的经济体中(货到付款占2015年全球支付的7%),任何代表在线支付的指标都会影响到电子商务指数。例如,在埃及大约90%的电子商务交易是通过货到付款支付的,而在最不发达国家,对现金的依赖更为明显(联合国贸易和发展会议,2017年)。

数据来源和国家覆盖范围

直到2016年,该指数使用的都是不同的支付指标计算的。2017年使用的指数计算方法,重新计算了前几年的得分以更好地说明变化。覆盖范围已经扩展到144个经济体,比2016年增加了7个。指数发生的变化总结在表17.1中。

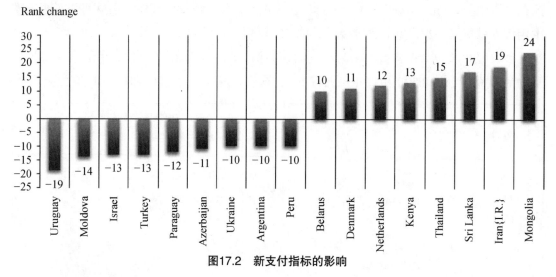

图17.2 新支付指标的影响

注：经济变化为±10。

资料来源：UNCTAD。

表17.1 联合国贸易和发展会议B2C电子商务指数的变化

2014年B2C电子商务指数	2016年B2C电子商务指数	2017年B2C电子商务指数
4项指标： ● 互联网用户 ● 安全的服务器 ● 信用卡普及率 ● 投递到家	4项指标： ● 互联网用户 ● 安全的服务器 ● 信用卡普及率 ● 邮政可靠性评分	4项指标： ● 互联网用户 ● 安全的服务器 ● 账户普及率 ● 邮政可靠性评分
130个经济体	137个经济体	144个经济体

该指数可用于估计在线购物的人口比例，可用于和官方发布的统计数据做对比。由于做了更改，2017版本数据显示出与在线购物人口比例有更高程度的相关性（见图17.3）。R^2值从2016年的0.73上升至2017年的0.79。

结　果

2017年贸发会议B2C电子商务指数排名前10位的经济体的信息如表17.2所示。卢森堡仍然表现最好。排名前10位的经济体中有6个也位居互联网购物者比例排名前10位的经济体之中。这表明指数中包含的变量和在线购物变量之间通常具有很高的解释性关联。在排名前10位的经济体中，韩国和日本的在线购物者实际比例低于指数预测值。这可能反映了指数中未包含的因素，例如偏好在实体店购物、缺乏信任和其他因素（贸发会议，2016

和益普索，2017）。值得注意的是，瑞士从第8位上升至第2位，英国从第10位上升至第6位，德国则从第14位上升至第9位。这些收益主要归功于邮政可靠性的提高。需要注意的是，排名前10位的经济体得分很密集，第1位和第10位之间的差异只有4个点。

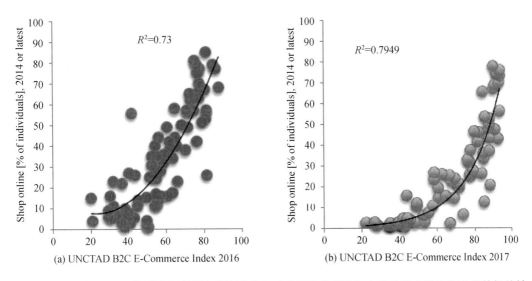

图17.3 2016年和2017年联合国贸易与发展会议B2C电子商务指数与在线购物人数比例之间的相关性

资料来源：UNCTAD。

表17.2 2017年联合国贸易与发展会议B2C电子商务指数排名前10位的经济体

2017年排名	经济体	使用互联网的个人份额（2016）	个人账户份额（15+，2014或之后）	安全的互联网服务器/100万人（标准化，2016年）	万国邮联邮政可靠性评分（2016）	电子商务指数（2016年的数据）	电子商务指数（2015年的数据）	指数排名
1	卢森堡	97	96	98	94	96.5	97	1
2	瑞士	89	98	100	99	96.4	94	8
3	挪威	97	100	96	93	96.4	95	3
4	荷兰	90	99	99	95	95.9	96	2
5	韩国	93	94	96	99	95.5	95	4
6	英国	95	99	92	95	95.1	93	10
7	瑞典	92	100	94	93	94.6	95	7
8	日本	92	97	89	97	93.8	94	9
9	德国	90	99	93	92	93.5	92	14
10	新西兰	88	100	90	95	93.3	93	11

资料来源：UNCTAD。

表17.3显示了按地理区域划分的平均值，区域差异很大。在互联网接入的情况下，非洲只有不到1/4的人口使用互联网，西亚则只有2/3，相对优势和劣势通常是不同的。东亚、南亚和东南亚需要提高互联网普及率，目前平均水平低于人口的一半，安全服务器数量也低于世界平均水平。在拉丁美洲和加勒比地区，互联网普及率与安全服务器数量都在平均水平，主要障碍似乎是邮政可靠性相对较差，账户渗透率相对较低。为了促进更具包容性的电子商务，非洲国家将尝试在所有政策领域追赶世界水平。

表17.3 2017年联合国贸易和发展会议B2C电子商务指数的区域值

区域	使用互联网的个人比例（2016）	使用安全的互联网服务器人数/100万人（2016年标准化）	UPU邮政可靠性得分（2016）	拥有账户的个人比例（15岁以上，2014年或最新）	联合国贸易和发展会议B2C电子商务指数值
非洲	23	31	31	29	28
东亚、南亚和东南亚	46	51	63	58	54
拉丁美洲和加勒比地区	51	57	34	46	47
西亚	67	59	50	56	58
转型经济体	64	59	66	49	59
发达国家	83	88	86	92	87
世界	52	56	54	55	54

根据万国邮联的说法，邮政可靠性得分的波动性有以下几种可能的解释：

（1）改进的跟踪事件和数据捕获（趋势通常是随着时间的推移获得更高质量的跟踪数据捕获）；

（2）随着电子商务相关物品的大量增长，一些国家引入了修订后的邮政流程；

（3）许多邮政网络可能遇到与电子商务量激增相关的瓶颈；

（4）许多国家的电子商务流量和邮政流量的构成可能已发生变化（例如运输和交付较重的货物和更昂贵的货物，导致更多的交货延迟），因此结果可能取决于最终交付给客户的产品或服务类型。

结 论

目前正在努力改善指数，并使其尽可能具有相关性。2016年，引入万国邮联可靠性指数得分。2017年，银行或移动货币账户的可用性使得它们取代了信用卡。2017年的指数的在线购物预测能力高于之前（见图17.4）。指数构成的变化总是意味着时间序列的中断。然而，2017年指数计算了两年的结果，这是一个时间序列的开始，随着时间的推移，各国将更好地衡量其在B2C电子商务推动方面的进展。

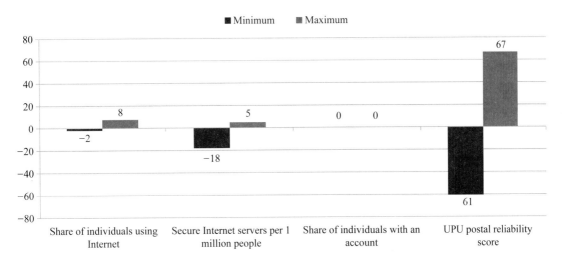

图17.4　根据贸发会议B2C电子商务指数，基于2015年和2016年数据，按指标列出的最小和最大变化值
来源：UNCTAD。

只有贸发会议B2C电子商务指数中的一些国家拥有在线购物的人口实际份额的数据。但是，现有数据显示各国之间的差异很大，从丹麦的80%到津巴布韦的1%不等。在许多发展中国家和转型经济体中，在线购物者仅占人口的一小部分；而在大多数发达经济体中，超过一半的人口在线购买商品或服务。